Finding Charity's Folk

RACE IN THE ATLANTIC WORLD, 1700–1900
Published in Cooperation with the Library Company of Philadelphia's Program in African American History

SERIES EDITORS
Richard S. Newman, Rochester Institute of Technology
Patrick Rael, Bowdoin College
Manisha Sinha, University of Massachusetts, Amherst

ADVISORY BOARD
Edward Baptist, Cornell University
Christopher Brown, Columbia University
Vincent Carretta, University of Maryland
Laurent Dubois, Duke University
Erica Armstrong Dunbar, University of Delaware and the Library Company of Philadelphia
Douglas Egerton, LeMoyne College
Leslie Harris, Emory University
Joanne Pope Melish, University of Kentucky
Sue Peabody, Washington State University, Vancouver
Erik Seeman, State University of New York, Buffalo
John Stauffer, Harvard University

Finding Charity's Folk

ENSLAVED AND
FREE BLACK WOMEN
IN MARYLAND

Jessica Millward

The University of Georgia Press
ATHENS & LONDON

This publication is made possible in part through a
grant from the University of California, Irvine.

© 2015 by the University of Georgia Press
Athens, Georgia 30602
www.ugapress.org
All rights reserved
Set in 10/13 Adobe Caslon Pro by Kaelin Chappell Broaddus

Most University of Georgia Press titles are
available from popular e-book vendors.

Printed digitally

Library of Congress Cataloging-in-Publication Data

Millward, Jessica.
Finding Charity's folk : enslaved and free black
women in Maryland / by Jessica Millward.
pages cm. — (Race in the Atlantic world, 1700–1900)
Includes bibliographical references and index.
ISBN 978-0-8203-3108-9 (hardcover : alk. paper) —
ISBN 978-0-8203-4878-0 (pbk. : alk. paper) —
ISBN 978-0-8203-4879-7 (e-book) 1. Folks, Charity.
2. African American women—Maryland—Biography.
3. Free African Americans—Maryland—Biography. 4. Faulk family.
5. Slaves—Maryland—Biography. 6. African American women—
Maryland—Social conditions—18th century. 7. African American
women—Maryland—Social conditions—19th century. 8. Slaves—
Maryland—Social conditions. 9. Slavery—Maryland—History—
18th century. 10. Slavery—Maryland—History—19th century.
11. Maryland—Biography. I. Title.
E185.93.M2M57 2015
305.48'896073075209033—dc23

2015023630

British Library Cataloging-in-Publication Data available

For Charity,

FOR BEARING ALL THINGS,

BELIEVING ALL THINGS,

HOPING ALL THINGS,

AND

ENDURING ALL THINGS.

—I CORINTHIANS 13:7

[African Americans] are the only folk so great in number who have added to their original racial possessions the language, the literature, the civilization, the culture, and the religion of an alien people. They seem a sort of crucible in which God is working out by experiment the problem of the adjustment of races.

—SHELTON HALE BISHOP, *The Romance of the Negro*

CONTENTS

Acknowledgments xi

Prologue: The Ghosts of Slavery xvii

INTRODUCTION Moving Freedom, Shaping Slavery: Enslaved Women in Charity Folks's Maryland 1

CHAPTER 1 Reproduction and Motherhood in Slavery, 1757–1830 14

CHAPTER 2 Beyond Charity: Petitions for Freedom and the Black Woman's Body Politic, 1780–1858 27

CHAPTER 3 Commodities and Kin: Gender and Family Networking for Freedom, 1780–1860 41

CHAPTER 4 Moving Slavery, Shaping Freedom: Households and the Gendering of Poverty in the Nineteenth Century 53

CONCLUSION Memorials and Reparations by the Living 67

Epilogue 73

Notes 75

Bibliography 95

Index 119

ACKNOWLEDGMENTS

As this book suggests, history plays an important role in maintaining families, and families play an equally important role in maintaining history. Bringing the Folks family into focus would not have been possible without the early lessons imparted by my maternal grandmother, Catherine Carter Dean. She taught me the importance of preserving one's family history and creatively uncovering the past when pieces are missing. My love for Maryland also has a connection to my grandmother through her niece, Debra, and her husband, Joseph Robert Sanchez Jr. (1953–2005). They introduced me to the wonders of Maryland and life on the Chesapeake Bay while I interned in Washington, D.C., during the summer of 1992. Later, they served as my hosts when I visited Maryland, listening as I reported my research highs and lows at the end of each day. When Debra moved back to Salt Lake City, their daughter, Sadie, opened her home to me. A chance conversation with Sadie also yielded a developing relationship with the Hampton Historic Plantation in Towson, Maryland.

I thank my fictive family in Las Vegas—Herb, Ora, Arial Ava, Lil' Herb and Isabel Dunson—for always welcoming me and for showing me love. To my immediate family—Gary, Miles, Jacqueline, Ashley, Lane, Melvin, Buddy, Maxie, Anthony, Alexis, Miley, Carter, and Cohen—I give my thanks and love. To my mother, Kathy, I thank you for doing the work to reconstruct our family's past while I was preoccupied with reconstructing Charity's. Thank you to grandmothers Irene Forbes Carter, Catherine Carter Dean, Reah Weatherston Millward, Clydies Wesley Finn, and Callie Perkins, who continue to watch and guide.

The descendants of Charity Folks willingly shared aspects of their family's history with me. Merle V. Bowser granted permission to reproduce documents related to Charity Bishop, the youngest daughter of Charity Folks. Dennis Dickerson of Vanderbilt University put me in contact with Dorothy Patton, a descendant of the Carey family of Chicago, who, in turn, put me in contact with Liberty Rashad, the great-great-great-great-granddaughter of Charity Folks. I cannot thank Liberty enough for her warm and enthusiastic support of this project. I thank those in Annapolis who willingly shared their time: Mark Leone of Archeology in Annapolis; Glenn Campbell of the Historic Annapolis Foundation; Janice Hayes-Williams of Our Local Legacy Heritage Tour; Orlando Ridout IV; and the late Orlando Ridout V and Barbara Ridout. To Joni Jones, director of the Banneker-Douglass Museum, I give a tremendous thanks. Who knew that meeting at a seminar table at UCLA would find us working on projects related to Annapolis's black past and to Charity Folks in particular.

Friends served as constant sources of support as I wrote. Thank you to Marianne Benztgen, Jessica D'Abreau Carlson, Ronald G. Coleman, Laurie Cooper, Francis Davis, Terence Fitzgerald, Roderick and Melissa Heard, Susan Henderson, Mikki L. Johnson, Kellie Jones, Jenny Kohler, Carol Leonard, Marcus Linden, Joseph Martinez, Anitra McMillon, Denise Oligney, Karla Padilla, Jeanna Penn, Joy Pierce, Adrian Pitts, Wilfred Samuels, Mike Santarosa, Sandra Siletto, Saskia Subramanian, Reggie Dean Sullivan, Edith Westfall, and Morrison, the incorrigible black pug. Thank you to Jewel Deane Moore and Timmy Kwakye for watching Morrison, for your prayers and advice, and for always inviting me to Thanksgiving and family reunions. A special note of gratitude to Marne L. Campbell for consistently standing in the gap: you are a true friend. For the sisterhood displayed by women of the Delta Sigma Theta Sorority, I thank Shawna Chambers, Neffisitu Dambo, Sherrika Ellison, LaShonna Harden, Amanda Henderson, Erica A. Hill, Jesse Knight, Mia Lavizzio, Marion L. Malcome, Nicole McCurry, Donna McIntosh, Jere Moore, Brianna Morgan, Regina Parnell, Brandi Simmons, and Carla Suber. The teaching of Pastor Kenneth C. Ulmer of Faithful Central Bible Church in Inglewood, California, and that of his son-in-law, Pastor Jody Moore of Praise Tabernacle Church in Chino Hills, California, sustained me throughout the process. To finish the race, I returned back home. Thank you to the members of the Westchester First Ward for supporting me in prayer and with acts of kindness. Barbara Stokes, thank you for the meals so that I could work uninterrupted.

Colleagues, staff, and students at the University of Illinois at Urbana-Champaign (UIUC) and later at the University of California, Irvine (UCI) contributed to the intellectual growth of this project. I apologize in advance if I left anyone out. I thank Jean Allman, Sharon Block, Merle Bowen, Ruth Nicole Brown, Antoinette Burton, Sundiata Cha-Jua, Bridget Cooks, Kirstie Dorr, Barrington Edwards, Alice Fahs, Karen Flynn, Rayvon Fouche, Doug Haynes, Kristin Hoganson, Fred Hoxie, Robin Jarrett, Sarah Clark Kaplan, Arlene Keiser, Craig Koslofsky, Chamara Kwakye, Clarence Lang, Cecelia Lynch, Minkah Makalani, Erik McDuffie, Marlah McDuffie, Megan McLaughlin, David Monje, Allison Perlman, Marc Perry, Diane Pinderhughes, Elizabeth Pleck, Dana Rabin, Sherie Randolph, Leslie Reagan, Kerry Ann Rockquemore, David Roediger, Ana Rosas, Emily Rosenberg, Vicki Ruiz, Nicole Rustin-Paschal, Sharon Salinger,

Jeanne Schepper, Kumi Silva, Damion Thomas, Brendesha Tynes, Georges Van Dan Abbeele, Tiffany Willoughby-Herard, Sheron Wray, and Fanon Che Wilkins. From January to October 2009, I participated in a lively writing group with UCI colleagues Rachel O'Toole and Nancy McLoughlin that enabled me to further crystallize my theories about enslaved women moving freedom across time and space. To the late Tom Sizgorich: I heard you. Though we lost you too early, I consider it a win to have known you.

I am deeply indebted to the history department staff members at both UIUC and UCI. Thomas Bedwell, the manager of the UIUC History Department, was vigilant in doing whatever he could to assist my scholarly production. Faculty and staff at the Illinois Statistical Consulting Office assisted in turning my crude math into statistical fact. Joy Bickham, the UCI history department financial officer, helped me to squeeze water from a rock during the tight UCI budget crisis of 2009–10. Conversations with students (many of whom are now colleagues in the profession) enrolled in my graduate seminars at both institutions contributed to the growth of this project as well. My students at UCI asked for weekly updates on the evolving story of Charity and her folk.

I treasure the friendship and scholarly questions posed by mentors, colleagues, and friends. I met Brenda Stevenson while enrolled as a master's student in UCLA's interdisciplinary program in Afro-American studies. I nearly committed to a project on curriculum instruction until I enrolled in her seminar on Family in the Slave South. She taught me to look for and read through the silences and pain of enslaved women. As my thesis adviser, dissertation chair, and friend, Brenda pushed me to find moments of joy in the lives of enslaved women while remaining attuned to the trauma of enslavement. Her questions—which continue to require on-the-spot answers—helped me become a better scholar. I honor her contributions to my development and thank her husband, James Cones (now my colleague at Irvine), and daughter, Emma, for their friendship as well. Dissertation committee members M. Edward Alpers, Ellen DuBois, and Belinda Tucker mentored me first as a doctoral student and later as a new colleague in the University of California system. Laura Edwards's seminar on Law and Society finally found a way into this work in the form of chapter 2. I continue to value her advice: "Don't lead the sources; let them lead you."

Ira Berlin was the first to read the dissertation as I began to turn it into a manuscript. I thank him for his candor and supportive correctives. Leslie Harris was kind enough to serve as my mentor during an Association of American University Women postdoctoral fellowship at Emory during 2006–7 and later served as a reviewer for the manuscript. Harris and series editor Richard Newman offered insightful advice on framing the study as well as page-by-page comments. Robert A. Goldberg read early chapters and alternated between cheerleader and conscientious objector. "Coach" Daina Ramey Berry read countless versions of what became this book, offering detailed comments and pivotal moments of prayer. Alan Galley provided advice on how to make this a biography without it being a biography. Akosua Perbi from the University of Ghana, Legon, communicated with me via e-mail about concepts of liberty among the Akan. I appreciate her willingness to canvas an array of experts on my behalf. Jean Allman and Dylan Penningroth helped to fill in whatever gaps Perbi and I missed. Thank you to Antoinette Burton, Karen Flynn, and Jennifer L. Morgan for reading nearly every word written in this book—this sentence does not do justice to the debt I owe you. Karen; her husband, Will Mitchell; and their son, Marshall, went over and above for me in the final stretch. They opened their home to me so I could write without distractions. Karen also constructed her own version of an academic boot camp, Writing on the Prairie, and recruited Maya Sanaa Brown, Ruth Nicole Brown, Sammer Jones, and Noreen Sugrue to join my village. Antoinette Burton—my colleague, former department chair, mentor, and friend—there is an elaborate jeweled diadem for you in heaven. To Jennifer L. Morgan, you are the consummate example of scholarly grace, and I continue to learn from you. The willingness of colleagues who served as conference chairs and commentators, informal readers, and sources of support is also appreciated. These individuals include Mumia Abu-Jamal, Rosanne Adderley, Luvvie Ajayi, Leslie Alexander, Mia Bay, Tage Biswalo, Eileen Boris, Brandi Brimmer, Christopher L. Brown, Tsekani Browne, the late Stephanie Camp, Marne Campbell, Camillia Cowling, Pero Dagbovie, Gneisha Dinwiddie, Stephane Dunn, Johanna Fernandez, Aisha Finch, V. P. Franklin, Jennifer Freeman, Tiffany Gill, Kali Gross, Evangeline Heiliger, Darlene Clark Hine, Maurice Hobson, Ronald Hoffman, Jessica Marie Johnson, Michael P. Johnson, Shannon King, Wilma King, Barbara Krauthamer, Suzanne Lebsock, Minkah Makalani, Valerie Matsumoto, Quincy T. Mills, Jennifer L. Morgan, Derek Musgrove, Sowande Mustakeem, Amrita Chakrabarti Myers, Peggy Pascoe, Rosalyn Terborg Penn, Dylan Penningroth, David Perez II, Leslie Schwalm, Loren Schweninger, Marie-Elena Smith, Ula Taylor, M. Belinda Tucker, Deborah Gray White, T. Stephen Whitman, Rhonda Williams, Stephanie Wright, and Karen Wulf. Noted scholars of the Chesapeake and Maryland history Lois Carr, Barbara Fields, Jean Russo, Lorena Walsh, and T. Stephen Whitman were equally supportive and approachable. A huge shout-out is reserved for the participants in the Faculty Success Program Summer 2013 and Summer 2014.

If the Maryland Historical Society was my second home during my dissertation, the Maryland State Archives served that role during my postgraduate write-up of this study. Robert Schoberlien, director of Special Collections granted me access to noncirculating collections. Senior archivist Robert Barnes shared his knowledge of local legal and genealogical sources. Maya Davis of the Legacy of Slavery in Maryland project was quick to respond to my research inquiries and shared items she found helpful. In addition, the research department responded to my long-distance requests for information when a research trip proved too far off. Margaret Burri and Cynthia Requart in Special Collections at Johns Hopkins; Becky Grundy at the Baltimore City Archives; Bea Hardy, formerly at the Maryland Historical Society; Joni Jones and Lynn Waller at the Banneker-Douglass Museum; Patrick Kerwin and Jeff Bridgers at the Library of Congress all graciously provided access to sources. Pamela L. Williams, manager of the City of Bowie's Historic Properties and Museums, answered my constant questions about Belair Plantation. Katherine Wilkins of the Virginia Historical Society was kind enough to share information on Anne Tasker Ogle. I thank curator Gregory Weidman, superintendent of the Hampton National Historic Site, as well as Gay Vietzke and archivist Julia Lehnert for granting me access to the Kent Lancaster Papers and other holdings at Hampton. Gregory Weidman allowed me work out of her office at various points, and Julia Lehnert continued to send me sources and references as she found them. Based on Lehnert's recommendation, ranger Vince Vance at the Fort McHenry National Monument and Historic Shrine invited me to participate in the National Parks Service's annual mid-Atlantic conference on slavery. I particularly thank Gail Silver, parish administrator at St. Philip's Church in Harlem, where Hutchens Chew Bishop and his son, Shelton Hale Bishop, served as rectors. Silver put me in contact with Bishop descendants, answered questions about the church's past, and granted me access to the St. Philip's collection at the Schomburg Center for Research in Black Culture, New York Public Library. Pamela Williams of the City Museums of Bowie answered my e-mail inquiries and shared Ogle/Tasker Estate inventories for Belair Mansion. She also put me in touch with Howard Ogle, President of the Ogle Family Genealogy group.

At the University of Georgia Press, Walter Biggins, Erica Armstrong Dunbar, Derek Krissoff, and Richard Newman assisted with editorial advice, kind words, and instructive criticism when necessary. Janet Abrahamson, Rachal Burton, Pamela Domash, Saron Ephraim, David Hageman, Montserrat Hansack, Chamara Kwakye, Melissa Salarin, Adam Thomas, and Carmen Thompson provided research assistance. Kate Babbitt, Carrie Crompton, Liana Krissoff, and Anne Rogers proofread the manuscript, related articles, and supporting materials. That their interest in the project pushed me to find answers is also appreciated.

Funding for this project came in the form of a Chancellor's Postdoctoral Fellowship in African American Studies at the University of Illinois, a University of Illinois Mellon Faculty Fellows release time grant, an Illinois Campus Research Board grant, an Association of American University Women postdoctoral award, the Maryland Historical Society's Lord Baltimore Fellowship, a Humanities Travel and Research Grant from UCI, and a Council on Research Computing and Libraries grant from the UCI Academic Senate. I also received financial support from UCI's Ghana Project, International Center for Writing and Translation, School of Humanities, and Advance program.

Upon finishing one of the most important versions of this study, I presented Charity Folks to students and staff and the University of Ghana, Legon. This was by far the most rewarding and spiritually fulfilling experience of my life. Charity Folks was home. I thank the faculty and staff of the Institute of African Studies as well as the Ghana Dance Ensemble. I thank Oh! Nii Sowah in particular for his vision. While in Ghana, I developed a special bond with other travelers. Thank you to Zahra Ahmed, Saron Ephraim, Darina Littleton, and Sylvia Smith for the crucial conversations about health and healing.

Finally, blessed be God's grace. *HIS* love restored the world of Charity and her folk so that we may all benefit from what they would have us know.

PROLOGUE

The Ghosts of Slavery

> But African memory does not disappear quietly into that good night.
> It mounts resistance in both the African continent and the diaspora.
> —NGŨGĨ WA THIONG'O, *Something Torn and New*

Charity Folks is a ghost of slavery who refuses to be silenced. She finds herself in the company of Margaret Garner's beloved daughter; the young girl known only as "Celia, a slave"; Sara Baartman; Sally Hemings; Sojourner Truth; Queen Nannie; and countless unnamed women who haunt historical memory because they carry the weight of the African diaspora's traumatic past.[1] Collectively and individually, their lives testify to the multifaceted legacies of enslavement and attempts by captives to dismantle the slave system without suppressing the system's most violent and horrific truths. The recovered pasts of enslaved black women underscore the competing interests involved in remembering, constructing, and commemorating their lives. Charity Folks is not as well known as the bondwomen mentioned, yet her story is equally compelling.

Charity Folks was enslaved in Annapolis, Maryland, and gained her freedom as an adult. An 1811 freedom certificate describes Folks as a "bright mulatto aged about fifty-two years," suggesting that she was born in 1759.[2] One local historian suggests that she was born at Belair Plantation, ten minutes outside of Annapolis, though no evidence supports this claim.[3] Thus, like many other enslaved persons, Folks's reconstructed life elicits questions whose answers seem to have been lost to history. What can be documented is that Folks lived the majority of her life as someone else's property. Despite the conditions into which she was born, she carved out freedom over the course of her lifetime.[4] She was manumitted in 1797, when she was approximately forty years old, and she made the most of her remaining years. By the time of her death in the early 1830s, Folks had amassed at least four properties in Annapolis.[5]

Charity gave birth to five children, all of whom gained their freedom. Her family line produced generations of "race men" and "race women," committed to uplifting African Americans.[6] Among her descendants are some of the most accomplished African American families of the nineteenth and twentieth centuries, the Bishops of Maryland and New York. During the nineteenth century, members of the Bishop family were prominent members of the free black class in Annapolis and Baltimore, serving as pillars of the Methodist and Episcopal Churches and fighting in the Civil War. During the twentieth century, the Bishops became pioneers in the fields of medicine and religion and participated in the ongoing struggle for black equality in America. Like other prominent families such as the Wrights, Bonds, and Grimkés, the Bishops struggled against slavery and helped lay the foundations for future generations of freedpeople, with ramifications into the twentieth century.[7]

I first encountered Charity Folks in 2000 while conducting dissertation research on slavery and manumission in Maryland's Anne Arundel and Baltimore Counties. She introduced herself through manumission documents executed by her owners in 1797 and 1807 that revealed that Folks secured freedom not only for herself but also for her children and grandchildren.

Folks's name and the fragments of her story quickly became the focus of a chapter in my dissertation, a book chapter I wrote, and later an article. She worked her way into every conference paper I presented for the next decade. Each new project I undertook reflected a deepening interest in Folks's life. Friends often asked me in disbelief, "Charity Folks? Is she still around?"

Indeed, Folks was present and unshakable, and my colleagues' comments challenged me to learn more about her—"Wouldn't it be great if you could tell the story of manumission through her eyes?" or simply, "There must be more." But it was not easy to find more; ten years after my first meeting with Folks, I knew only of the two manumission documents related to her and of one article by another historian that briefly mentioned her.[8]

The details of Folks's life eluded me, and a friend suggested that I change my relationship to the project, reminding me that I became a historian to reclaim the lives of those viewed as insignificant. I changed everything: my approach, my assumptions, my anxieties, and my language. Not surprisingly, I also stepped beyond the archive. I was not sure of my new path, but I was open to what lay ahead.

When I moved from archive to memory, history started to unfold in real time. I contacted Glenn Campbell, senior historian at the Historic Annapolis Foundation. He had no specific details but remarked fondly, "Oh, Charity," and put me on the path to learning more about her life after manumission by providing me with the names of some noted Annapolis historians and scholars. Dr. Mark Leone of the Archeology in Annapolis project at the University of Maryland shared knowledge about his archeological digs around the home of Folks's daughter, Little Charity, and her husband, William Bishop. Leone suggested that I contact a local historian of black Annapolis, Janice Hayes-Williams. She responded to my inquiry with enthusiasm, assuring me that Folks's life did not end with the two documents I held in my hand.

Campbell, Leone, and Hayes-Williams encouraged me to contact the descendants of John and Mary Ridout, Charity's owners. I wondered how best to approach this task. Does one simply write an e-mail or initiate a phone call saying, "Excuse me for intruding, but I am interested in your ancestors who owned slaves"? Holding my breath, I did just that. First I contacted Orlando Ridout V (1953–2013), chief of the Office of Research, Survey, and Registration at the Maryland Historic Trust. I asked about any details he could provide on Charity Folks, her family, and her role in the Ridout household. He replied that although he had no primary source information on Charity Folks, he could show me the Ridout house on Duke of Gloucester Street, where the enslaved Folks had lived for many years. She worked in the house and tended to the needs of family members and tenants occupying the adjacent row houses that John Ridout had built for his children and one of which was at that point home to Orlando Ridout V. He invited me to stop by for a visit the next time I was in Annapolis.

Within two weeks of my e-mail and phone conversations, I found myself in Annapolis on a rainy afternoon in November 2009. Hayes-Williams gave me a walking tour of the city and clarified facts about the Folks family. She also accompanied me to the Ridout home. Orlando Ridout V and his wife, Barbara, welcomed me into their home. They allowed me to take pictures of their yard, the site of the once-famous Ridout garden, and to ask questions about Folks.[9] We digressed a bit as we exchanged stories about our recent trips to Africa—mine to Ghana, Ridout's to Gambia. He encouraged me to speak with his father, Orlando Ridout IV. Lannie Ridout was as outgoing and helpful as his son, and less than a week after we first spoke on the phone, he met me in the lobby of the Maryland State Archives. We talked for nearly two hours about Folks, the Ridouts in England and Maryland, and the American Revolution. He provided critical insight into crop cultivation at Whitehall, the Ridout family farm, and shared his experiences as a historian, first as a walking tour guide of Annapolis beginning in 1937 and later as the director of the Maryland Historic Trust. Ridout assured me that I should not be concerned with finding "everything": what needed to be revealed would be revealed in its own time.

I asked him if there was an aspect of Folks's life that he would like to see explored. He emphasized his interest in the friendship between her and his ancestor, Mary Ridout. I also asked whether any family narratives mentioned Folks. He responded that Folks had been largely forgotten until Joan Scurlock, one of Folks's descendants, began researching her family's genealogy. In 1999, a year before the manumission document found its way into my project, Scurlock had written an unpublished family history about the descendants of Charity Bishop, or Charity Jr., as Hayes-Williams and Scurlock referred to her.[10] When Lannie Ridout and Hayes-Williams mentioned the existence of this narrative, I sensed that the answers I had been searching for were finally within my reach. Scurlock had passed away several years earlier, but her narrative inspired me to approach my own research with newfound vigor.

Approaching Folks's descendants proved more challenging than contacting the Ridout family. I had become accustomed to thinking of the Folks family's history as "my research." How would the family perceive my interest in her story? I needn't have hesitated—they were welcoming.

In 2013, I published "Charity Folks, Lost Royalty, and the Bishop Family of Maryland and New York," in the *Journal of African American History*. Though I was pleased with the evidence I uncovered, I was bothered by some lingering holes in the story. Jean Russo, formerly of the Maryland State Archives, helped me to fill in these gaps. Russo was invaluable in helping me re-create a world that Charity Folks would recognize. I also listened to the silences, which were often more revealing than the evidence, requiring me to think about how history is documented, how it is remembered, and how it is imagined.

Charity Folks remains an obscure historical figure, perhaps because Annapolis has received less attention from historians than its neighbor city, Baltimore. To date, enslavement in Maryland is associated almost exclusively with three figures: Kunta Kinte, the Gambian stolen from Africa in 1767 and immortalized in Alex Haley's best seller, *Roots*; fugitive slave and abolitionist Frederick Douglass; and abolitionist and Civil War scout Harriet Tubman.[11] *Roots* is commemorated by a statue of Alex Haley on the Annapolis dock. Plaques and memorials honor Tubman in Dorchester County, where she was born, and in Albany, New York, where she lived in her later years. In 2013, a seven-foot statue of Frederick Douglass was unveiled at the U.S. Capitol building to commemorate the Emancipation Proclamation.[12] The Frederick Douglass–Isaac Myers Maritime Park offers walking tours of the Fell's Point area of Baltimore, where Douglass lived.[13] The fact that Douglass fled the city in 1838 and did not return until after the Civil War is not highlighted in the tour.

As a manumitted woman, Charity Folks is more representative of the enslaved experience in Maryland than Kinte, Douglass, or Tubman. Folks did not flee bondage, like Douglass and Tubman; die enslaved, like Kinte; or end her life in poverty, like Tubman.[14] Folks and her family were like forty-five thousand other enslaved people in Maryland who gained their freedom in the decades following the American Revolution.[15] This small geographic region boasted a remarkably fluid population of free, enslaved, and quasi-free blacks. Folks lived her entire life in the Chesapeake, but she inhabited all three zones of freedom over the course of her lifetime.

My research into Folks's life forced me to confront the challenges of historical memory in recovering African American women's lives. Perhaps more than African American men, African American women were elided by the experience of bondage. Relatively few black women wrote narratives of freedom, and fewer still are the focus of major biographies or autobiographies. Moreover, scant historical material exists on enslaved black women.

As a social history, this book challenges scholars to restructure their methodologies for doing black women's history in early America. This methodology orphans neither the African nor the enslaved past. It imbues all aspects of African American women's lives with meaning. It is important to distinguish between the life of Charity Folks and what her life symbolized.

Reconstructing Folks's life also meant trying to understand her pain—a historic pain born out of social conditions, legal policies, and popular constructions that were antiblack, antiwoman, and for the most part anti-black-women. Only by experiencing this pain can one truly write about and understand the redemptive and revolutionary nature of black women's joy. As generations of black women can attest, rejoicing is the key to surviving.

And perhaps greater than joy is the work of peace. As Folks's example suggests, the enslaved are persistent in their desire to be remembered. They beckon to be seen as more than names and prices jotted down in plantation account books. They invite us in through artifacts, oral history, and photos. They challenge us to engage in the "untelling" of narratives that neglect their pain, their suffering, and even their triumphs. Their ongoing presence forces society to deal with the flesh-and-blood diaspora involved in the trafficking of bodies.[16] They call for attention. They call for apologies. They call for atonement. How we choose to engage the enslaved past, then, is not simply a matter of discourse. We honor enslaved women's call to be remembered by telling their stories and speaking their names. Re-creating their lives not only provides a better understanding of humanity but may also bring peace to their souls.

Historians assume that they choose their subjects. The main part of this book (chapters 1–4) reflects my decision to study Charity Folks and other women like her. The chapters present evidence and put that evidence in dialogue with other scholars. Yet the book is also about what happens when the subject picks the historian. The prologue, conclusion, and epilogue of this study detail my experience with this process. This book merges these two types of narratives into a portrait of black women (and families) in slavery and freedom in early national Maryland.

Maryland may have been atypical in the early 1800s, with its growing free black population, but it was not unique. Its mid-Atlantic neighbors—Virginia, Pennsylvania, and Delaware—also experienced great jumps in black freedom, with African American women serving as key players in the transition. Despite much recent work on African American women, we still know much less about their lives, experiences, and roles in shaping freedom in early national Maryland. This book consequently brings attention to black women's experiences of slavery and freedom in the eighteenth and nineteenth centuries.

Finding Charity's Folk

INTRODUCTION

Moving Freedom, Shaping Slavery
Enslaved Women in Charity Folks's Maryland

> Though I speak with the tongues of men and of angels, and have not charity, I am become as sounding brass, or a tinkling cymbal. And though I have the gift of prophecy, and understand all mysteries, and all knowledge; and though I have all faith, so that I could remove mountains, and have not charity, I am nothing.
> —I Corinthians 13:1-2 (KJV)

This book draws its inspiration from the life of Charity Folks, an enslaved woman from Annapolis, Maryland, but it is more than a biography. It uses the fragmented archive of Charity Folks's life as a window into the ways in which slavery, freedom, and liberation intertwined in African American women's experiences. In particular, it explores how enslaved women moved across and beyond the boundaries between slavery and freedom and ultimately changed those boundaries. In the decades following the American Revolution, enslaved women such as Charity Folks acquired freedom by being granted it by their owners, petitioning for it, negotiating for it, and buying it.[1] By accessing manumission, enslaved women shifted the boundaries of freedom in terms of the law, their communities, their families, their work, and even their own bodies.

For enslaved African American women, freedom, like enslavement, was tied to the womb. Enslaved women such as Charity were mothers either willingly or unwillingly; however they became mothers, they envisioned lives that included their families. Their reproductive abilities were used to perpetuate the slave economy, and finding loopholes in the law could mean that they could give birth to free children. In studying the life of Charity Folks, I have looked at more than fifteen hundred manumission records, certificates of freedom, plantation letters, journals, and runaway slave advertisements spanning archives in the United States, Great Britain, and Ghana. These documents demonstrate that manumitted women in cities such as Baltimore, Charleston, and New Orleans hastened the South's transition into a quasi-free society. As Loren Schweninger's research attests, women were manumitted in greater numbers than men, represented a larger portion of the free black population, and controlled a significant percentage of black wealth.[2] Camillia Cowling's work on Cuba shows that manumitted women were crucial to the transition from a slave society to a free one.[3] The example of Charity Folks shows that though we tend to see manumission as an individual act, achieving freedom was a communal effort for enslaved women. The routes to freedom were varied and often took several generations to traverse.

Personal expressions of freedom among enslaved people could be found in nearly every aspect of chattel bondage—being truant from the plantation for a period of time, resisting sexual exploitation, choosing whom to love. But legal freedom—the rights to move freely, get an education, choose one's occupation, earn a living, own property, and pass on one's assets to one's children—was always a dream and in some cases was a goal. Most enslaved people never realized such legal freedom before the passage of the Thirteenth Amendment, which ended slavery, and the Fourteenth Amendment, which declared African Americans citizens, but every successful bid empowered more bondpeople to seek it for themselves and their loved ones.

Charity's case and the wider social histories allow us to expand existing definitions of *freedom* and *independence* in revolutionary America by understanding the varied meanings these terms held for bondwomen. The gendering of freedom influenced notions of liberty, equality, and race in what became the new nation. This gendering also had long-term implications for African American women's interactions with the state. While a singular definition of freedom—or its manifestations—is not really possible because the conditions and experiences of enslavement were not uniform, this study focuses chiefly on two aspects of how enslaved people defined freedom. The first is grounded in the historically specific circumstances of enslaved women, exploring their experiences and suggesting ways that using the archive of Charity's life can move our discussion of the lives of enslaved women and their long struggles for freedom in new directions. The second involves an investigation of the meanings of mobility and its impact on the autonomy of enslaved and ex-slave women's lives. I turn first to the problem of freedom within historical circumstances.

African American Women and the Problem of Freedom in the Age of Revolution

The social histories of slavery that emerged in the post-civil-rights era suggest that manifestations of freedom were both temporally and ideologically wedded to the Age of Revolution (1775–1832). Some argue that the American

Revolution constituted the first successful slave rebellion in the United States.[4] In the 1960s, Benjamin Quarles's *The Negro in the American Revolution* presented the most thoroughly researched study on the subject. Quarles argued that the American Revolution was a watershed moment for the eighty thousand to one hundred thousand blacks who took up arms with the British or fled when the British departed. Where Quarles differed was in his argument that African Americans fought for freedom, not for the American republic.[5] If Quarles can be faulted for anything, it is that he ignored black women in his discussion, which was not unusual, given the invisibility of enslaved women in early discussions about slavery. Motivated by this silence, Mary Beth Norton notes that the American Revolution held different implications for African American families.[6] To further interrogate the impact of the War of Independence, Jacqueline Jones notes in a pivotal article that the American Revolution meant something entirely different for enslaved women than it did for the white men or black men who took up arms.[7] Finally, masterful works by Sylvia Frey and Cassandra Pybus provide a much-needed overview of the role of African American resistance in the American Revolution by highlighting women's experiences alongside those of men.[8]

Erica Armstrong Dunbar was the first to focus on African American women's experiences in the North during the early republic.[9] Dunbar's emphasis on enslaved women in Philadelphia fills a gap in our understanding of how emancipation not only shaped the North but also served as an indicator for how African American women in other locales experienced freedom. Catherine Adams and Elizabeth Pleck's work on New England highlights how women such as Elizabeth Freeman interacted with a patriarchal structure and sued for their freedom.[10] Most recently, Afua Cooper's example of Angelique, an enslaved woman who set fire to Montreal, shatters the notion that moments of revolution and rebellion were the exclusive province of the white founding fathers of the United States or of Toussaint L'Ouverture, the leader of the Haitian Revolution.[11]

Of course, studies of enslaved women owe an intellectual debt to Deborah Gray White's *Ar'n't I a Woman? Female Slaves in the Plantation South*. At the time of its initial publication in 1985, White's book was among a small though significant number of works focusing on slave women's experiences in the United States.[12] At the heart of White's study was the argument that life in bondage fostered an alternative definition of womanhood for African American women.[13] In the wake of White's work, scholars have pursued the challenge of historicizing feminist consciousness among African American women in the context of the variety of historical conditions that slavery helped to create. Scholars of African American women's history pay particular attention to the role community plays in feminist agendas. Leslie Alexander suggests that "it is impossible to remove Black women (or the study of Black women) from the context of the entire Black community."[14] Thus, not surprisingly, emerging studies of black women and feminism highlight the role of the community in studies of such varied topics as slavery, church participation, and welfare reform. Moreover, scholars face the analytic challenge of interrogating issues of race, gender, and feminism not only in local contexts but also at the global, national, and transnational levels.[15] Scholars also pay particular attention to the reality that multiple definitions of black feminisms exist temporally and spatially.[16]

This book takes up these issues by examining the agency exhibited by African American women as they laid claim to social and economic power via recourse to the law, and it explores the impact of that agency on their identity construction in the postrevolutionary period. Following the American Revolution, Africans and African Americans borrowed from the language of the War of Independence to further articulate their own claims to freedom. The lives of Folks and others of her generation suggest that those who actively sought their freedom occupied a stressful social position even after manumission. The difficulties women faced as they sought and gained legal freedom while simultaneously working to maintain family ties illustrate the gendered nature of emancipation.[17] In the case of Charity Folks, gaining freedom required a long and patient battle. Nearly forty years elapsed between the time she was promised freedom and her grandchildren's liberation. Like many other enslaved women of her time, she was the architect of her own freedom.

Place and the Difference It Makes

Prior to the Civil War, nowhere was the growth of a free black population more apparent than in the city of Baltimore, where those numbers multiplied nearly twentyfold between 1790 and 1860.[18] The rise of the free black population in Baltimore was not unique, however. Like Jennifer Hull Dorsey, Max Grivno, and Calvin Schermerhorn, I explore manumission in other areas of Maryland that also had large free black populations.[19] Slavery and freedom had coexisted in Maryland since its founding. During the revolutionary era, manumission laws fell in step with rhetoric that slavery was contrary to the word of God. After the war, manumissions rose in Maryland for a range of reasons: the influence of antislavery religious denominations; the sincere appeal of egalitarian theology; the decreasing profitability of slavery as a source of labor; changing county laws; individual slaves' personal (and at times sexual) relationships with planters; and enslaved individuals' negotiations for their freedom.[20]

Maryland's geography and topography also influenced the surge in manumission. As Barbara Fields notes, tobacco, the primary crop cultivated by bondpeople, surrendered its dominant position in the state in the late eighteenth and early nineteenth centuries. Tobacco production, which had constituted 90 percent of Maryland's agricultural crop in 1747, declined to 14 percent by 1859.[21] By the middle of the eighteenth century, wheat had replaced tobacco, and other types of work done by bondpeople were increasingly diversified and divided more along gender lines.

Place as both a political and geographical boundary also shaped access to manumission. Anne Arundel County, home to the state capital, Annapolis, and Baltimore County, which at the time included the city of Baltimore, were separated on the east–west axis by the Chesapeake Bay but adjoined to the north.[22] According to the first U.S. Census, in 1790 approximately 10,130 enslaved blacks resided in Anne Arundel County. The enslaved black population remained small and relatively unchanged over the next forty years, numbering 10,347 in 1830, as a consequence of natural reproduction and the region's continued participation in the domestic slave trade.[23]

In contrast, the free black community of Baltimore County and particularly Baltimore City mushroomed during this era. The county's slave population burgeoned, while a free black wage-earning population emerged. In 1790, Baltimore County had 7,132 enslaved persons, with that number rising to 10,653 by 1830. Much more dramatic, however, was the increase in the free black population: the Census counted 927 free blacks in the county in 1790 and 17,888 in 1830. Many blacks, both enslaved and free, worked in the developing port of Baltimore City, which became, to borrow Christopher Phillips's phrase, "freedom's port."[24] Yet the port also became an important thoroughfare for those engaged in the domestic slave trade.

As a result of these demographic changes, enslaved and free persons could look across the mighty Chesapeake or even to the dwelling next door and see a society that contrasted with the one they knew. Black families, whether enslaved or free, lived in a world of contradictions. Free blacks witnessed the realities of enslavement daily, and enslaved men and women often worked alongside free blacks and were aware that they were being paid for their labor. Freedom produced contrasting experiences, depending on one's social location. Charity Folks's position in the Maryland capital generally and the Ridout home more intimately meant that she experienced the Age of Revolution (1763–1823) from a variety of vantage points.[25] She heard about the black uprisings in Saint-Domingue from bondpeople whose owners resettled in Maryland. She probably served their owners when they called on the Ridouts and voiced their opinions about how the themes of liberty, equality, and fraternity were fine for the French but held dangerous implications when espoused by blacks. Folks also lived through the denouement of the revolutionary era, the War of 1812. She died sometime in 1830, as the Jacksonian emphasis on the common man was on the ascent. Her vision of freedom, while informed by a multiplicity of sources, nonetheless remained centered on one goal—the release of herself and her family from slavery.

If place is important for the history of freedom's meanings for African American women, it did not fully determine how they lived. How enslaved women reacted to their circumstances is just as important as where they lived. Indeed, the question of agency looms large in histories of manumission, though as a practice, agency is notoriously hard to quantify. In his 2003 essay "On Agency," historian Walter Johnson argues that an overemphasis on agency threatens to minimize the brutality that surrounded lives of the enslaved. Johnson is especially critical of the notion that scholars could "give" a subject agency instead of understanding subjects as agents a priori. Johnson argues that overemphasizing historians' "discovery" of black humanity inadvertently supports the hegemonic assumptions about black inferiority that scholars want to negate.[26] Despite the cogency of his argument, scholars have remained divided on the issue of agency. Max Grivno and Amrita Chakrabarti Myers, for example, point out the limits of agency. As Myers argues, for free black women, agency existed somewhere between life choices and the legal apparatus. Therefore, when women were faced with real-life situations, "agency had its limits."[27] The idea that agency has its limits should be heeded. It certainly applies to the life of Charity Folks. While earlier generations of scholars have noted that enslaved domestics were more privileged than other laborers, Thavolia Glymph and others demonstrate the constant power struggle between enslaved domestics and their enslavers.[28] And Folks was enslaved as a domestic house servant for the majority of her years. When she was manumitted, two of her children remained in bondage, testifying to the significance of Damian Alan Pargas's argument that "agency should not be confused with success."[29] The laws of a slaveholding society ultimately undercut black women's agency. For recently manumitted women, Myers argues, "the reality of their lives indicates that absolute power is as much a myth as absolute freedom."[30] Indeed, the coupling of agency and autonomy has the potential to produce a version of "freedom" that constructs an experience that would have been largely unrecognizable to enslaved and manumitted people.

This study of Charity Folks and the worlds she inhabited uses agency, resistance, and their dialectical relationship as conceptual tools for investigating the complex historical reasons for the capabilities—and incapabilities—of African American women in this period. The women in this study remind us that challenging slavery meant a constant battle that included the real potential for defeat; nonetheless, they prepared for the fight using whatever weapons could be found in their arsenal.

Enslaved people were acutely aware that the family was not only their greatest source of strength but also their greatest vulnerability.[31] Individual challenges to power had profound implications for family and community networks both in slavery and in freedom. Bondwomen knew that any individual act on their part might have decisive effects on their families. The decision to strike an overseer might mean being sold and separated from loved ones. Likewise, one's freedom or that of a family member might cause family rupture. Familial love could motivate enslaved women to challenge slavery but it could also limit those challenges, leading to concepts of independence that were communal rather than individual.

Historians must ask several questions about the factors that seem to have affected bondpeople's bids for freedom. First, did gender matter? The answer is yes. Enslaved women were often freed at the end of their childbearing years, meaning that how and when manumission occurred helps us to understand enslaved family and community dynamics. Second, how did one's privilege on the plantation shape access to freedom? This study answers this question by showing the diversity of manumission experiences. And third, did color matter? Yes, although not always in predictable ways.

Enslaved women pushed back against their condition by refusing to submit to sexual exploitation, physical abuse, grueling work, and extended periods of time away from family and friends. Such gestures, whether they resulted from agency or resistance, underscored a determination to survive. Enslaved women thus directly defied the laws put in place to regulate African American life. "Freedom" as a concept and as a reality was integral to the lives of bondmen and bondwomen.[32] Freedom shaped the context of slavery; likewise, slavery shaped the context of freedom.[33] Slavery and freedom in the life of Charity Folks were not mutually exclusive. But for her and many others, mobility played a large role in shaping both the meanings and experiences of freedom. I now turn to this "moving history."

Occupation, Hiring, and Mobility in the Making of Manumission and Freedom

Simply by moving through space, enslaved women actualized moments of autonomy in their daily lives. On the few occasions when she was able to visit with her son, Frederick Douglass's mother traveled nearly thirty miles round trip. Harriet Tubman's mother was hired out to another owner several times a year. And each week, Charity Folks moved among agricultural, urban, maritime, and industrial spaces.[34] She haggled with local farmers about their produce, discussed the price of fish and oysters with watermen on the dock, and traded medicinal herbs and roots from the Ridout garden for other goods. Able to move about with a measure of autonomy, Folks was part of a larger world of free and enslaved African Americans with whom she could share news and information. Like many enslaved women, she witnessed freedom before actually experiencing it.

Though we know little about the details of how she navigated that world, we do know how occupational mobility shaped enslaved women's sense of autonomy in the context of late eighteenth-century Maryland. The majority of enslaved people in cities such as Annapolis and Baltimore lived in or near their owners' residences, usually with two to four other enslaved people.[35] Some lived in lofts or closets in their masters' houses, while others "lived out" in small shacks in the alleys directly behind their owners' homes.[36] Those who lived out occupied cramped quarters, yet they experienced more freedom of motion than those who lived inside owners' homes. That distance created opportunities for mobility.

According to the 1798 tax list, one black woman and one enslaved child lived at the Ridouts' Annapolis house.[37] It is not clear who this woman was, but it may have been Folks and one of her children. Her other four children may have lived either at Whitehall, the Ridout country home seven miles outside Annapolis, or at other Ridout farms in various parts of the countryside. Folks may have been able to visit her children when her work for the Ridouts took her to these properties.

Movement was always gendered, as was the work of the enslaved. Historians Ira Berlin and Philip D. Morgan observe that "when, where, and especially how [bondpeople] worked determined in large measure the course of their lives."[38] Enslaved women labored as cooks, domestic maids, seamstresses, and wet nurses in the homes of their owners. Those who possessed midwifery skills had considerable range of motion in the wider neighborhood as well.[39] On Baltimore County's Hampton Plantation, enslaved women labored in agricultural trades such as wheat cradling.[40] Bondwomen traveled from the country residences of their owners when their knowledge of spinning and weaving was needed in the city. They also worked in their owners' shops and as hucksters in urban markets. The shift from tobacco to wheat in the late eighteenth century, Baltimore's increasing urbanization, and the Chesapeake waterways meant that movement became a defining feature of the lives of the area's enslaved people.[41] Though Charity Folks was enslaved in the Ridouts' Annapolis home, she frequently bought supplies for the Ridout family at Annapolis stores and occasionally traveled with those who owned her.

Charity Folks's African heritage provided her with knowledge about the healing power of roots and herbs.[42] The Ridout garden contained agents such as peppermint and spearmint—used to cleanse spaces to enable connections with the spiritual world—as well other herbs and roots known for their spiritual and physical healing powers.⁴³ She not only used plants from the P[...] her own practice as a healer but traded them with others, re[...] medicinal agents in return.⁴⁴

Industrial slavery moved enslaved women from one space [...] were sent to work alongside men in the iron forges and furnaces [...] Maryland's countryside, among them Baltimore County's Northampton Furnace and Ironworks, owned by the Ridgelys; the Baltimore Ironworks, owned by the Carrolls, Carters, Dulanys, and Taskers; and Anne Arundel County's Snowden Ironworks, owned by John Snowden.⁴⁵ Women enslaved by Maryland governor Charles Ridgely worked at the Northampton furnace in a variety of capacities: Lucy Smith and Charlotte Smith carried coal, Mary Ashburn stocked coal, and Deborah Lee oversaw the "washing" of coal to clean it of salt and rock.⁴⁶ Some women worked as lime burners, miners, and molders.⁴⁷ Work in the iron forges was the most dangerous of all the labor done by enslaved men and women.⁴⁸ Many women who worked in the iron forges lost limbs or carried the evidence of accidental burns in the form of scars. Charity did not labor in a forge or furnace, but she would have known people who did. The Ridouts were associated with or related to some of the most prominent furnace owners of the time.

Industrial slavery provided enslaved men and some women with opportunities to earn wages. Bondpeople at the Northampton Forge often received wages for their work, and if they produced more than their quota, they were paid for "overwork."⁴⁹ Unlike outwork, for which owners received the profit for work done by the enslaved, overwork was paid directly to the enslaved. Men had more opportunities for overwork than women and were more likely to accumulate cash through this type of labor. Nevertheless, industrial slavery also strained families when members were away from home for long and often indeterminate lengths of time.⁵⁰

Plantation women who were sent to the labor market in cities such as Baltimore worked in close proximity to free blacks and immigrant whites and perhaps gained a new perspective on the worth of their labor. Frederick Douglass observed a "marked difference" between his experiences as a slave on an Eastern Shore farm and as a laborer in the bustling urban center of Baltimore.⁵¹ He noted, "A city slave is almost a freeman. He is much better fed and clothed and enjoys privileges altogether unknown to the slave on the plantation."⁵² Douglass noted that Baltimore in particular served as a beacon of hope for some slaves who wished to at least temporarily escape the plantation setting.⁵³ Cities also provided enslaved women with the opportunity to participate in the market economy, often as small-scale consumers on behalf of whites.⁵⁴ The market space also provided market women or hucksters with the opportunity to enjoy some income. In Baltimore, for example, hucksters sold goods for their owners and received a portion of the earnings.[55] Some also sold vegetables from their private garden plots. Fortunate market women used these funds to buy their freedom, though this phenomenon was less common in Baltimore than in Charleston, South Carolina, and New Orleans. However, like women in those cities, Baltimore market women continued to sell goods in the market after they were freed.

Though there is no evidence to suggest that Charity was ever a hireling, she would have come in contact with enslaved hirelings. Hirelings often had marketable skills that translated into profit for their owners. They were also hired out to learn trades so their owners could use their skills on their own holdings. Enslaved women occasionally were manumitted while they were hired out. In January 1814, for example, Joseph Corbel Martiner entered a Baltimore court to grant freedom to his slave woman, Arsene, who was living in Norfolk, Virginia, in exchange for one dollar. He testified that she was "28 and able to work and gain a sufficient livelihood."[56] Children were more likely to be manumitted with their mothers than with their fathers. For example, among the 1807–50 manumission records that listed men and women freed with offspring, only two males were mandated to provide for their children, compared to sixty-one females.[57]

For enslaved black women, travel also resulted from changes in the white household. Charity Folks's husband, Tom, for example, was sold during the American Revolution when his owner, Lloyd Dulany, returned to England.[58] Some historians have suggested that Charity Folks came to the Ridout house as part of Mary Ogle's dowry when she married John Ridout.[59]

The capacity—and determination—of enslaved people to move expanded the parameters of freedom within slavery. Despite the fact that their mobility was limited, monitored, and criminalized, enslaved people found ways to move among neighboring plantations, and the ability to move through the landscape allowed bondpeople to build community.[60] One man recounted, "We would meet on the bank of the Potomac River and sing across the river to the slaves in Virginia and they would sing back to us."[61] Others benefited from "working socials," gatherings during harvest time to complete a particular task.[62] If enslaved people were already mobile, exaggerated fears of an impoverished free black class affected decisions about whether to manumit bondpeople.

When freeing slaves, owners assured county officials that the former slaves would not become wards of the county or the state. In 1784, the Maryland state legislature authorized manumission by wills regardless of age if the slave could provide proof of sufficient livelihood.[63] Similarly, in 1790, An Act Related to Freeing Slaves by Will or Testament stated:

> Provided always, that no manumission hereafter to be made by last will and testament, shall be effectual to give freedom to any slave or slaves, if the same

shall be in prejudice of creditors, nor unless the said slave or slaves shall be not exceeding the age of fifty years, and able to work and gain a sufficient maintenance and livelihood, at the time the freedom to be given by last will and testament shall be intended to commence.[64]

As this example indicates, age was a very important factor in manumission. Lawmakers were concerned that elderly manumitted blacks would not be able to provide for themselves. Likewise, laws suggesting that slaves could be freed if they could "gain a sufficient maintenance and livelihood" worked to ensure that freed blacks would not become dependent on county welfare systems such as the orphans' court.[65] Given enslaved people's informal mobility, these statutory provisions may be seen as defense mechanisms against full-fledged freedom and total mobility once manumission was secured. To the extent that they had informal mobility, Charity and her folk possessed agency even before they were legally freed.

Moving through History with Charity Folks

Whether mobile or stationary, enslaved women called on the spiritual world to affect their lives in bondage. Archeological surveys done in the late twentieth and early twenty-first centuries have revealed the complex belief systems of enslaved people in Annapolis. Spiritual caches were discovered under the floorboards at Slayton House, the middle unit of three row houses adjacent to John Ridout's home initially built as homes for Ridout's children and guests. The caches were placed together on east–west and north–south axes at the center of one room, composing a cosmogram.[66] Some African ethnic groups believed that cosmograms offered believers protection over long periods of time.[67] Though this particular cosmogram dates from after Folks's death, archeologist Mark Leone suggests that enslaved blacks practiced Yoruba-influenced religions, and he provides evidence showing that two bondwomen at the nearby home of Charles Carroll were responsible for taking a red shift and other items that went missing.[68] Combined with other materials, the missing items might have made an effective altar or shrine to the orisha Shango.[69] Enslaved women welcomed contact with the Most High, with lesser deities, and with their ancestors, probably relying on all of them to help order life. Indeed, African spiritual practices blended with elements of Christianity to enable many enslaved women to withstand and at times transcend the horrors of their environment. Charity Folks was enslaved in a Methodist household; she lived across the street from Catholics; her descendants were and are Episcopalians. Her own religious experiences blended the Old World with the New.

Buying freedom was complicated. Owners often agreed to one price but raised it over the days, months, and years the enslaved person needed to raise the funds. In some cases, enslaved persons paid more for their freedom than their owners had paid to purchase them. At the same time, the movements of trusted servants and hirelings expanded their circles of family, friends, and neighbors. Bondpeople met freeborn and manumitted blacks while running owners' errands or traveling to places of hire, all the while expanding their social and informational networks. Folks's mobility expanded her world well before she was promised freedom. Her movement from slavery to freedom became possible in part because of her dutiful services to her owners. However, being rewarded for faithful service was only one part of her quest for freedom. In Folks's case, freedom meant a long and patient battle. Nearly forty years passed from the time she was promised freedom until her grandchildren were liberated. Though their paths were buried among private negotiations and oral histories, enslaved women must be seen as architects of their own freedom. Freedom was not bestowed on them; they worked for it.

The analysis in the chapters that follow centers on the roots and routes enslaved women navigated in their quest of freedom. Chapter 1 examines how bondwomen stretched the boundaries of slavery and exercised what autonomy was available to them as mothers. Bondwomen lived in constant fear of sexual exploitation and a range of physical and psychological abuses. Interracial sex was a form of violence, and for enslaved women, bondage meant rape or the threat of rape. This chapter investigates how enslaved women's sexual experiences shaped their choices, their sense of identity, and the ways they reared their children.

Whereas the previous chapter centered on moving freedom within slavery, the remainder of the book focuses on how slavery was remade in freedom, building on Saidiya Hartman's concept of the "afterlife of slavery."[70] How did enslaved women move from slavery to the "afterlife" of slavery, and how did they deal with this reality? Chapter 2 investigates the relationship between enslaved women's bodies, freedom petitions, and manumission laws. It takes as its point of departure Maryland's 1809 Act to Ascertain and Declare the Condition of Such Issue as May Hereafter Be Born of Negro or Mulatto Female Slaves, which minimized age requirements for freeing enslaved children.

Chapter 3 returns to Charity Folks's life and the extent to which her experience was both typical and exceptional, focusing on manumission and extended family networks. In no other place is the coexistence of slavery and freedom more visible than in some African American families. American independence was profoundly shaped by the ability to move not just freedom within slavery but also slavery into freedom.

Chapter 4 returns to the notion of family by focusing on free black households—specifically, those of Folks and her children. Because women were often freed with their children, hereditary slavery, manumission, and social responsibility were intertwined. Manumitted women used institutional mechanisms, such as apprenticeships, to maintain their children's free status.

Pinpointing when and how female-headed African American households developed is not an idle exercise. Debates surrounding Senator Daniel Patrick Moynihan's 1965 report, *The Negro Family: The Case for National Action*, still resonate. Moynihan's report suggested that households headed by black females, which had their genesis in slavery, had fostered the underdevelopment of black America.[71] Moynihan's findings challenged scholars of African American life to account for the present condition of black America and to defend the varied compositions of black families. The ensuing dialogue called into question to what extent the state was responsible for the creation and perpetuation of the female-headed black household. The epilogue returns to the topic of Charity Folks and the ghosts of slavery as a sort of prescription for understanding the totality of black women's experiences.

For enslaved women, freedom was multifaceted. The ability to move between the spaces of slavery and freedom sustained families even in the midst of forces determined to keep them enslaved. Unearthing the world of Charity Folks and women like her provides contemporary scholars with another lens through which to view the black freedom struggle. This "rebirth" of Charity Folks and her world enables us to delve deeper into the complexities of Maryland history by revisiting the concept of the middle ground and stretching it beyond geographical space to understand generational relationships to bondage and liberation.

CHAPTER I

Reproduction and Motherhood in Slavery, 1757–1830

> And whether one member suffer, all the members suffer with it;
> or one member be honored, all the members rejoice with it.
> —I Corinthians 12:26 (KJV)

Motherhood under slavery was the farthest thing from freedom. During the late eighteenth century, the power of mothering came to the forefront in the form of the moral mother. The moral mother was white, privileged, and dedicated to instructing her children about how to be productive citizens. In this role, white women suffered from gender oppression, as their day-to-day lives often fell short of the ideal. However, their struggles were nothing compared to that of enslaved women. Enslaved women were considered property, meaning that there was a fiscal value attached to the most intimate of processes, the birthing of a child. Sasha Turner notes that when Britain ceased participation in the Atlantic slave trade, planters in Jamaica altered punishment and labor regimes for enslaved women.[1] Camillia Cowling's work on Cuba suggests that reproduction served as the site of freedom.[2] Differing colonial models aside, scholars agree that giving birth under slavery meant reconciling one's own role as a reproducer of the slave system with the joys and heartbreaks associated with pregnancy.

Attention to the private and intimate worlds of enslaved women is essential for excavating bondwomen's resistance to everyday slavery, because women's history does not merely add to what we know; it changes what we know and how we know it.[3] Indeed, the true stakes of enslaved resistance resided somewhere in the quiet spaces, often outside of that which could be archived. This chapter, then, is particularly attuned to resistance and agency as it relates to enslaved mothers. By investigating reproduction and motherhood through agency and resistance, this chapter argues that although enslaved women did not possess legal power, they used whatever tools were available to carve an area of freedom in their life. How did enslaved women socialize their children in the midst of the horrors of slavery? How did those who were exploited sexually by their masters develop strategies to help their children avoid the same fate?

Many studies suggest that sex with their owners often resulted in certain privileges for bondwomen and their children. Indeed, the evidence that the manumitted children of such interracial encounters comprised a noteworthy proportion of elite free black communities is strong.[4] But interracial sex was but one path that enslaved women used as an avenue to freedom. To complicate the narrative of interracial sex as an avenue to freedom, I examine enslaved women's sexual relationships with both white and black men, reproduction, and motherhood to ask what these three categories have to do with freedom.

Black women's enslavement included exposure to rape or the threat of rape; the knowledge that the most intimate of acts made them breeders, multiplying the enslaved population; and the heartbreak of separation from partners or children. Sexualized violence was a common form of physical punishment and psychological torture.[5] Difference was coded on the enslaved African body, and whites' perceptions about black women's morality were distinctly different from those about white women.[6] Slaveholders' notions about black women's sexuality were quite literally inflicted on enslaved women's bodies. Sexual experiences, pregnancy, and childbirth forced enslaved women to reconcile intimacy and violence, the pain of slavery and the joy of motherhood.

Motherhood held the potential to be revolutionary. Slavery and freedom intersected at motherhood as women instructed their biological and fictive children on how to behave; how to respond to physical and sexual violence; and how to dream, if they dared to do so. Women taught their children strategies of resistance. Children learned to avoid drawing undue attention to themselves. Daughters learned to avoid white men and overseers at any cost as well as the heartbreak of losing a loved one as a consequence of circumstances beyond their control. The range of sexual experiences and reproductive realities reveal that despite difference, enslaved mothers used all available resources to protect themselves and their families. Parenting provided space in which to pass on stories and traditions to assist one's descendants as they negotiated a life in and (ideally) out of slavery.

Birthing Children in Slavery

Early laws of colonial America reveal planter dependence on the natural reproduction of the enslaved population. In 1662, the Virginia state legislature determined that racial chattel slavery would be a permanent, inheritable condition by asserting that the status of the child followed that of the mother. If the mother was enslaved, so too were the children, regardless of the status of the children's father.[7] This law ensured that children of free black men and enslaved women as well as children of free white men and enslaved women faced a lifetime of enslavement and barred children descended from white men from laying claim to their fathers' free or Christian status. Similar laws developed throughout the South during the late seventeenth century, all of them upholding the notion that whiteness equaled freedom and blackness equaled slavery.[8]

Sex between slave owners and enslaved women was openly practiced, but sex between black men and white women was forbidden. Late seventeenth-century law privileged white male authority: whereas the 1662 Virginia law upheld a slaveholder's power to engage in relations with enslaved women, a 1664 Maryland law criminalized relationships between white women and black men.[9] A white woman who married a black man was declared a slave for the duration of the life of her spouse. Legalized slavery was also extended to the children of black men and white women, who were to be enslaved regardless of the children's age. Thus, interracial relationships had legal consequences for those excluded from the power structure.[10]

Laws specifying slavery as a permanent, inheritable condition represented one end of a spectrum of statutes that governed the status of those with African ancestry. At the other end of this spectrum were laws that stipulated the conditions under which enslaved individuals could gain their freedom. Manumission laws initially developed in the early Chesapeake so that slaveholders could free children they had fathered with bondwomen. As wage labor began to replace slave labor, planters used manumission as a means of relieving themselves of the costs of maintaining a permanent enslaved labor force.[11]

By the middle of the eighteenth century, New World planters relied on natural reproduction rather than on imports to replenish their chattel population. As slave traders and owners realized the importance of women in reproducing the enslaved population, the nature of African chattel slavery was transformed.[12] Because slavery was permanent and inheritable through one's mother, slaveholders expanded their dominion to inside the bodies of enslaved women.[13]

Reproducing an enslaved population meant that enslaved women formed families willingly or unwillingly. Birth rates among the black population of what would become the United States were higher than rates in the Caribbean, where planters actively discouraged the nuclear family.[14] American slave owners encouraged enslaved people in places like Maryland to form families so that as the enslaved population grew, so did the owners' wealth in human capital.[15]

The recognition that women's reproductive labor was a site of future wealth attuned slaveholders to methods for assuring the birth of healthy children. Sowande Mustakeem notes that the health of enslaved persons during the Atlantic Middle Passage was a priority, not only to protect the value of the cargo but also because keeping the enslaved healthy meant that the crew of the ships transporting Africans to the New World would not succumb to disease.[16] The attention to the health of the enslaved gained greater importance as abolitionist sentiment grew. Sasha Turner suggests that the end of British participation in the international slave trade significantly altered the work lives of enslaved women in Jamaica.[17] Cut off from one source of new laborers, planters protected another source by protecting the health of pregnant women by varying their work assignments and degrees of punishment. For example, some believed that whipping a pregnant woman caused fewer complications if the woman lay over a hole in the ground so that her belly was protected from the lash. Marie Jenkins Schwartz argues that by the nineteenth century, slaveholders protected their investments in current and future slaves by paying formally trained doctors to deliver the children.[18]

Maryland slaveholders valued highly fertile women, and their sale could bring in cash. In 1772, Maryland planter Francis Ware sold eight enslaved people, two of them "breeding women."[19] Conversely, planters hesitated to purchase women who were not perceived as fertile. In 1780, Cornelius Conaway, the overseer at John Galloway's Tulip Hill plantation, doubted that they should buy "Billy's wife" because although she was a "strong young wench," he did not "know that she will breed."[20] A month later, Conaway repeated his anxiety: "Sims wants to part with his wife in exchange for [Billy]. I have wrote before. I don't think that Billy's wife will have children."[21]

Yet while slaveholders' commonly equated a bondwoman's worth to the children she could bear, enslaved women found that practice traumatic. Enslaved in Texas, Rose Williams was confused when she learned that she had been paired with fellow bondman Rufus to make "portly children" for her owner.[22] Williams did not understand that "marriage" for enslaved people often meant breeding more bondpeople for the ruling class regardless of the partners' feelings for each other.[23] Such experiences indicate how for women, the painful reality of reproduction in slavery meant sleeping with men they had not chosen for themselves.

The binary between enslavement and freedom was constructed through the rape of enslaved women. White men could legally marry white women and at the same time force themselves on enslaved women. By failing to criminalize the rape of black women, the laws of slaveholding supported violations of enslaved women. Legislation also erased evidence of bondwomen's intimate relationships with enslaved men. In 1767, Maryland attorney Daniel Dulany argued that enslaved women and men were legally "incapable of civil marriage" because they were property.[24] Assumptions about the normativity of white relationships vis-à-vis those of the people they owned stood at the center of the paradoxes of slavery. African Americans were subjects under the law only to the extent that their existence held up the institution of slavery.

The embodied history of enslaved women as property and as mothers meant that they lived in a world where sexual violence was legally sanctioned. The rape of bondwomen was well known in white and black communities. Former Maryland bondman James W. Pennington remembered that his owner purchased a girl for "no honorable purposes."[25] But enslaved women are largely invisible in the rape cases presented in court since violating an enslaved woman was not a crime. Sharon Block suggests that rape cases in early America hinged on the notion of consent—but only for white women.[26] Enslaved women lacked legal personhood and indeed human attributes and thereby fell outside legal definitions of rape.[27] Notions about black women's sexuality, then, were worked out on enslaved women's bodies.[28]

Enslaved women suffered from other forms of violence not only from male slave owners but also often from their wives. According to Thavolia Glymph, white women were the "female face" of slave owners' often-violent power.[29] Former slave Richard Macks observed that "black women have had many hard battles to fight to protect themselves from assault by employers. They were subjected to many impositions by the women of the household through woman's jealousy." Macks remembered a doctor "who bought a girl and installed her on the place for his own use; his wife hearing of it, severely beat her."[30] The condition of enslaved women worsened when wives felt threatened or when relationships developed between male slave owners and their female chattel. Countless enslaved women were sold when their owners' sexual interest provoked jealousy from the slave mistress.[31]

Enslaved women raised children and tried to hold onto a semblance of family in a world stacked against them. The fate of their children and grandchildren was determined through the practice of entail. Entailing the future increase of enslaved women was one way that masters ensured that their female heirs, whose financial inheritance was usually far less significant than that of male heirs, would own property.[32] When she was about twenty-five years old, Baltimore County bondwoman Anne Maria and her children became the property of Mary Cook when Cook's father died.[33] Thomas Bond of Baltimore County deeded to his sister, Jenet Fen, "the labour, work and service of a certain Negro Phoebe and her increase." Fen was counseled to clothe and provide for Phoebe and her children, and upon Fen's death, those slaves were willed to another female family member.[34] The death of an owner often resulted in the entailment or manumission of enslaved women's future children.

Enslaved mothers in Maryland had no legal recourse when their children were entailed or funneled to the Lower South through the secondary slave trade. However, many bondwomen found ways to defend themselves from oppression.[35] As mothers, black women tried to instill in their children a brighter vision of freedom.

Resistance and Childbirth

The story of slavery cannot be told without addressing resistance. Indeed, the story of slavery is the story of resistance itself. In the early colonial period, some slave women used medicinal herbs and roots—indigo, rue, tansy, cotton root—to prevent or terminate unwanted pregnancies because slavery violated their cultural practices.[36] Sarah Levering remembered that two bondwomen in her hometown, Baltimore, "were unwilling to breed slaves for any master."[37] Some bondwomen committed infanticide rather than watch their children endure enslavement.[38] Such acts generally occurred in secret and are thus absent from the historical record, but women who were caught were usually sold.[39]

Accused of killing her daughter rather than allow her to be returned to slavery, Margaret Garner typifies the extreme nature of motherhood. When asked if she was out of her mind when she killed her daughter, she responded, "No I was as cool as I am now and would much rather kill them then have them ripped apart by piecemeal."[40] Most acts of resistance were less violent, but many enslaved mothers shared Garner's desire to protect their children at any cost.

Hard work, inadequate diet, and disease contributed to high infant mortality rates among slaves. Such conditions, combined with oppressive psychological factors, may have reduced women's desire to procreate.[41] Barbara Bush attributes Caribbean slave women's low fertility rates to tensions inherent in their dual roles as mothers and workers, which both consciously and unconsciously influenced slave women's responses to childbirth.[42] Maria Cutrafelli argues that these factors contributed to a "dread of motherhood" that sometimes prevented women from conceiving children.[43]

No matter what wounds black women suffered or how secretive they were forced to become with the outside world, they could not live in isolation. Deborah Gray White writes, "Not every black woman was a Sojourner Truth or a Harriet Tubman. Strength had to be cultivated. It came no more naturally to them than to anyone.... If they seemed exceptionally strong it was partly because they often functioned in groups and derived strength from numbers."[44] Forging a female community and drawing strength from extended family could not erase the pain and trauma associated with gendered violence; it could, however, help in surviving the experience.

Motherhood and Enslaved Families

Motherhood was a biological condition, an emotional relationship, and sometimes, as a result of separation or sale, a category that was to be erased all together. Even as slaveholders clarified the connection between racial slavery and reproduction, the psychological and emotional realities of enslavement left many mothers without children. What role, then, did mothers play in building and creating families? In his memoirs, Frederick Douglass observed, "Slavery does away with fathers, as it does away with families. Slavery has no use for either fathers or families and its laws do not recognize their existence in the social arrangements of the plantation."[45] Historians believe that Douglass's father was his mother's owner, but slavery also erased her from his life: he saw his mother, Harriet Bailey, only a few times during his youth at Wye Plantation in Maryland. When they did exist, however, enslaved families were perhaps the most important—and most fragile—institution in the African American community.

Scholars of slavery agree that enslaved men's and women's ability to forge families and communities served as a key survival mechanism across the generations.[46] Yet mothers were the parents most present in the lives of young slave children.[47] Women typically resided in matrifocal families with extended and fictive kinship networks.[48] By the nineteenth century, slaves' marital patterns and family structures were extremely complex: some slaves maintained serial marriages on the same plantation, while others maintained "abroad marriages," in which the husband and wife lived on different plantations.[49]

Like families, marriages were fragile. Enslaved people could be married only if their owners consented to the union. Born enslaved in Charles County, James V. Deanne had "seen many slave weddings," with participants jumping the broom and dressing up as much as possible for their special day.[50] Wedding ceremonies, however, did not ensure marital success for African Americans when one or both of the individuals were enslaved. Slave marriages were subject to pressures based on sales and temporary separations initiated by owners and overseers.[51] However, owners also recognized that sales could bring families together, potentially benefitting their masters if it helped keep bondpeople quiescent. In the midst of financial difficulty, John Hurt asked John Galloway to buy some slaves, among them "a Negro woman with 3 children, whom has a husband at [Galloway's] Eastern neck plantation." He assured Galloway that the bondpeople were sound and were being sold solely "for want of money."[52] Families occasionally were sold together. In 1815, Thomas Randall's executors sold off "a Negro woman and child" to raise cash to settle debts.[53] Galloway sold Sue and her three children to Robert Thomas for seventy-five pounds.[54] Other owners sold slaves away from their families, apparently with few qualms. Thomas Ringgold, Galloway's brother-in-law, wrote, "I forget to inform Mrs. Ringgold that Mrs. Thompson wants to take the Negro girl on the terms offered. What they were, I do not know. I understand it was one of Frank's children."[55] Ringgold's recognition of the child's family, rare in the archives of slave sales, is even more unusual in that it refers to the child's father rather than his mother.

In other cases, however, owners explicitly sought to keep families together even when doing so caused financial disadvantage. At the death of Benjamin Tasker Sr., executors attempted to finish the process of property distribution that had begun at the passing of Samuel Ogle nearly twenty years earlier. When faced with selling bondpeople at Tasker's Enfield Chase Plantation, Daniel Dulany noted, "I could not think of separating husbands and wives and tearing young children away from their mothers." According to Dulany, the sale went well, but the prices "would have been higher if the Negroes had been set up separately." Many of the hands were of prime value, "but as they are in families will sell at a disadvantage."[56]

Historians argue that enslaved families were more likely to be stable in Maryland than further South, since the relatively small number of slaves in the border state resulted in stronger kinship ties.[57] Sixteen family lines were noted among the three bondpeople owned by Charles Carroll of Carrollton, Maryland, but the presence of multigenerational families on the plantation should not obscure the fact that individual members were sold away, particularly after Carroll's death in 1832. Emily McTavish, Carroll's granddaughter and the executor of his estate, authorized the sale of Adolpheus, but Carroll's son intervened, writing to a local attorney, "Mrs. McTavish has sold Adolpheus to Georgia and he was taken hence in irons and is now at Woalfolks [a Baltimore slave trading house]. His wife, who accompanies my servant Joice, is in the greatest distress for she is much attached to him." Carroll pleaded with his attorney to "arrest the sale of him. Find someone to buy man and wife."[58]

Enslaved mothers who were lactating had a better chance of keeping their children with them. The estate inventory for Richard Sprigg's West River Farm in Anne Arundel County, noted nine mother-child relationships among the seventy-eight slaves.[59] Bet, Suck, and Flora had "suckling" children, several of them between four and five years of age. Though this status may have enabled these women to stay with their children at the time of the estate's division, there was no guarantee that they or their children would not subsequently be sold or otherwise separated. Slave women could not anticipate all of the ways that circumstances might prevent her from protecting her children no matter what strategic alliances she might make.

Parenting as Resistance

Enslaved resistance was methodical and calculated. Delores M. Walters notes that enslaved women's responses to gendered violence—whether threatened or realized—were based first on critiquing and then on transforming systems of oppression.[60] Charity Folks was born in 1759 to Rachel Burke, an enslaved woman. At least one of Burke's and Folks's descendants believes that

Burke was enslaved twenty miles west of Annapolis at the Belair Plantation, which would mean that Burke was owned by Maryland governor Samuel Ogle until his death in 1752, when she passed to his brother-in-law, Colonel Benjamin Tasker.[61] However, Burke does not appear on any lists of Ogle's or Tasker's slaves, so there is no way to substantiate this belief.[62] Likewise, little documentary evidence supports the idea that Tasker—a politician, a businessman, a slave trader, and a bachelor (and quite possibly homosexual)—fathered Charity.[63] If Tasker indeed was her father, she was little more than three years old when he died in 1760, so any information she gleaned about him would have come through memories passed down by others. Her parentage was likely well known in the slave community and probably whispered among members of the Ogle and Tasker families.

The slave quarters of Belair have not survived, yet a public display at the mansion suggests that enslaved people made their home in the cellar of the grand mansion.[64] Charity Folks may have lived the first ten to twelve years of her life in the cellar at Belair with her brother, James, and their mother, or she may have lived in Annapolis. Folks likely entered the Ridout household between 1765 and 1767, though it is unclear how she did so. According to family lore, John Ridout acquired her when he married Samuel Ogle's daughter, Mary. Rachel Burke's family appears to have been together for a brief time before Rebecca Tasker married Daniel Dulany and Anne Tasker married Samuel Ogle. However, if Folks belonged to the Dulany family, as her brother did at one time, she may have been purchased when she was in her early teens, finding herself on the cusp of puberty in a house with a mistress she knew and a master she did not. John and Mary Ridout's sons, Samuel and Horatio, were abroad for much of her adolescence, but Folks was not necessarily free from sexual violation, coming into close contact with John Ridout and his visitors. Burke might have anticipated her daughter's situation and explained that if she could not avoid sexual exploitation, she should use it to her advantage.[65]

Living outside the normative definition of womanhood forced enslaved mothers such as Burke to nurture the spirits of their daughters in response to the psychological damage and physical abuse that encircled their lives.[66] These mothers passed on advice about how to avoid sexual violation: "Kick, [and] if you can't kick, bite."[67] They told stories of bondwomen who refused marriage to men not of their choice: in 1638, one black woman in New England responded to attempted sexual coercion not only by refusing to have sex with the man but by announcing that she "had been a Queen in her own Country."[68] They shared triumphant narratives of women who wounded their aggressors and others who castrated and killed their abusers.[69] Rachel Burke and Charity Folks were part of a community of bondwomen who used a variety of womanist strategies to oppose their exploitation.[70] Burke would have taught her daughter to fashion an identity within the limited choices available to her and thus laid the crucial foundation from which Folks drew as she matured to adulthood.[71]

Parents taught resistance by modeling behavior for their children. Former Maryland bondman Samuel Ringgold Ward remembered when his mother, Anne, challenged the severe flogging of her husband and railed against the owner "in pretty strong language." Instead of whipping or selling Anne, the owners threatened to sell Samuel as soon as he reached a healthy weight and size. The owners assumed that the threat of being separated from their child would subdue the enslaved couple; instead, these parents responded by running away and taking the child.[72]

In such instances, parenthood led to a sense of purpose and possibility for enslaved mothers and fathers. Despite slave owners' efforts to reduce childbearing to a simple act of expanding their wealth, enslaved women and men attached emotional meaning to birth and child rearing. Ward's parents exemplify parenting as a form of resistance.

Enslaved women at times chose to use sexual relationships with owners to gain better treatment, material goods, or freedom. In New Orleans, manumission and the plaçage system developed hand in hand: through that system, an owner could "place" an enslaved mistress in a residence he provided for her. Through manumission, he could make her a free woman. The plaçage system and the fact that Spanish and French colonial laws made it relatively easy to manumit slaves produced a large free black class both before and after the Louisiana Purchase of 1803. Some Louisiana planters appear to have delighted in attending social functions with their black mistresses while their white wives pretended to be oblivious. Others participated in the "fancy trade," in which slaveholders purchased women for the purpose of sexual gratification.[73] Emily Clark reveals that plaçage was much more complex than historians initially believed.[74] The image of the mother of color encouraging her daughter to engage with a wealthy white man was a myth. White planters responded to the Haitian rebellion by crafting a mythological submissive black woman who contrasted with the rebellious and vengeful revolutionary.[75]

Annapolis and Baltimore were not New Orleans, but that does not mean that enslaved people were oblivious to the possibilities embedded in their connections to the slaveholding society. Enslaved people gathered what details they could about their families and passed the stories to successive generations. Frederick Douglass deduced that his father owned his mother: "My father was a white man. He was admitted to be such by all I ever heard speak of my parentage. The opinion was also whispered that my master was my father."[76] Some Baltimore African Americans still maintain that they are descended from an enslaved woman and Charles Ridgely, the owner of Hampton Plantation.[77]

The Anne Arundel County manumission records for 1780–1850 offer very little empirical evidence to indicate that sex with an owner presented an avenue to freedom in that county. Nevertheless, the phenomenon may still have existed. Enslaved at Riversdale Plantation in modern-day Prince George's County, Eleanor Beckett bore five children by George Calvert, her owner, beginning in 1790. In 1799, Calvert married socialite Rosalie Stier; he then arranged for Beckett to marry a male slave. Calvert apparently maintained some sort of relationship with Beckett, and in 1801, he freed her and five of her children. Over the next twenty-five years, Calvert returned to court several times to reaffirm their free status as well as that of her grandchildren, ultimately freeing twenty members of her extended family. After his wife's death in 1822, Calvert moved Beckett and her family to Montgomery County, Maryland.[78] We have only a limited ability to know the context and details of such long-term relationships between enslaved women and slaveholders, but we must assume that Beckett and other women calculated the risks and possibilities of using sexual connections to negotiate manumissions.

Little is known about Beckett outside of what can be gleaned from manumission records, but her history has reverberated down through the generations: her present-day descendants in Montgomery County recount the family's origins at Riversdale.[79] Even as her memory is preserved, many questions about the substance of her relationship with Calvert remain. Was her first sexual experience with Calvert traumatic? Did she put up a fight? Or did she resign herself to the reality that sexual violation was inevitable and sleep with him in exchange for certain favors? She might have calculated that giving birth to her owner's slave child while enslaved would be no more difficult than giving birth to a free child if she were manumitted. She might truly have loved Calvert, and he might have reciprocated. Yet as Kathleen Brown reminds us, interracial sex always existed somewhere between coercion and choice, and the relationship was never one between equals.[80]

Despite the secrecy involving interracial relationships, some white men were very public about their relationships with enslaved women. Irish immigrant William Bishop Sr., known as "Daddy Bishop," began a relationship with Jane Minsky while she was enslaved. Family narratives suggest that they met while Minsky worked in an Annapolis hotel/tavern owned by her enslaver. Generations of the Bishop family have maintained that the relationship was not based in violence. Contemporary family members wonder about the extent to which the relationship began consensually.[81] Bishop eventually bought and freed Minsky, yet the children she birthed while enslaved remained in bondage, in accordance with local law. Bishop could not buy and free his children until they reached the age of self-sufficiency. He undoubtedly worked out agreements with other owners, as at least two of his children were freed when they reached the age of twenty-one. A schoolteacher by training, Bishop began a carting business when employment as a teacher proved unsuccessful. What was initially considered a demotion eventually provided a lucrative income. When his black son, William Bishop Jr., was manumitted at the age of twenty-one, he inherited the carting business from his father.[82]

Not every slaveholder found manumission of children to be a viable option. Thomas Jefferson had difficulty reconciling his role as a slaveholder with his role as the father of enslaved children. Annette Gordon-Reed suggests that Jefferson was conflicted about manumitting his enslaved children because of his persistent paternalistic belief that Africans and African Americans were not suited for freedom. While Jefferson never manumitted Hemings, his will freed their three sons. Hemings negotiated for the manumission of their children at the expense of her own freedom, a difficult task that reveals the lengths to which mothers would go for their children's freedom.[83] Unlike Jefferson, however, Bishop did not own slaves and was not part of the landed gentry.

Manumission laws provided a narrow gate to freedom for mothers and an even narrower gate for their children. Manumissions were granted on an individual basis and never jeopardized the balance of power, which positioned the laws of the slaveholding South as an omnipresent force in the lives of African Americans. Manumission laws were slaveholders' laws, and any space in which a slave could gain freedom was a loophole, not an open door. However, the ability to negotiate one's freedom and that of one's kin became a very important vehicle of resistance for enslaved women. Women who sought manumission considered how best to secure freedom for their families. Some shrewd and deliberate enslaved women maximized their relationships with their owners to provide a better future for themselves or their children.

We do not know how many enslaved women who used sexual relationships with their owners to achieve their own manumission or that of their children. It is clear, however, that enslaved women's ability to bend the boundaries of slavery depended on how they responded to the perpetual violence encircling their world. Enslaved women knew that they, their bodies, and the children they birthed, regardless of parentage, were inextricably linked. They passed on stories of their experiences and those of other women; they reconciled themselves to the gendered violence they faced as well as squared off against it.

For some, freedom came in the form of manumission. Rachel Burke was manumitted without a court transcript as an adult, though there is a manumission document for her son, James; in 1789, Burke paid Anne Ogle sixty pounds to free him.[84] Burke appears in one other historical document: a family member noted in a court transcript that she was living in the 1820s, well into her eighties.[85] Her daughter, Charity Folks, birthed at least five children in slavery:

Harriet Jackson (b. 1780), James Jackson (b. 1786), Hannah Folks (b. 1787), Mary Folks (b. 1788), and Lil' Charity Folks (b. 1793).[86] She would have been twenty-two years old when Harriet was born—slightly beyond the usual age of first birth for a bondwoman.[87] Charity Folks ultimately negotiated freedom for her children in the sort of unrecorded transactions that were far more common than formal legal manumissions.

Folks's eldest children, Harriet and James, bore the surname Jackson, though she apparently never used that name and it does not appear on any slave inventories for the Ridouts, Taskers, or Ogles.[88] Nor was Jackson a prevalent surname among Annapolis residents either black or white. Folks's descendants believe that Jackson was either a bondman who ran away or a free black who died soon after James was born, though it is more likely that he was a slave who was forcibly separated from Folks and their children.[89]

Much more is known about Thomas Folks, who apparently fathered Charity's youngest three children. He was owned by John Davidson, a shopkeeper and tavern owner, and maintained an "abroad" relationship with Charity. Folks acted as a father to all five of Charity's children, and he and Thomas and James spoke often about various matters concerning the family.[90]

Charity and Thomas Folks's ability to begin and maintain their family testifies to the adaptability and complexity of kin relationships in slavery. Another free black woman gave birth to Thomas's son, Henry, in 1789, less than two years after Hannah Folks's birth.[91] Only Lil' Charity resided with her mother at the Ridouts' home in Annapolis. According to the 1783 Annapolis tax list and the 1790 U.S. Census, one enslaved woman and one enslaved child resided in John Ridout's home.[92] It is reasonable to assume that Charity's other four children lived either at Whitehall, the Ridout country home seven miles outside Annapolis, or at one of the other Ridout farms in various parts of the Maryland countryside.

Charity Folks spent some time with her children, but their interactions were limited. When her duties required her to travel among the Ridout properties, she could visit her children, but her primary responsibility was to the Ridout family, not her own.

Reproduction yielded few legal freedoms for women, yet their descendants used the courts to articulate their claims to freedom based on their maternal lineage. Enslaved women and their descendants moved their negotiations for freedom into the public arena of the court. As chapter 2 discusses, enslaved women also filed formal petitions so that they and their children could enjoy life in freedom.

CHAPTER 2

Beyond Charity
*Petitions for Freedom and the
Black Woman's Body Politic, 1780–1858*

> And even things without life giving sound, whether pipe
> or harp, except they give a distinction in the sounds,
> how shall it be known what is piped or harped?
> —I Corinthians 14:7 (KJV)

Enslaved women were keenly aware that freedom, like slavery, was tied to their reproductive labor. Regardless of the constraints and violence, enslaved women envisioned a life that included family. For that reason, their visions of freedom were deeply related to their identity as mothers, meaning that they pressed tirelessly to leverage freedom for themselves and their children. Women whose fragmentary genealogies are preserved in court records speak volumes about historian Loren Schweninger's assertion that oral genealogy played a central role among enslaved black women.[1] This chapter looks beyond the particular case of Charity Folks, asking how enslaved women used legal loopholes to advance their claims to freedom. The case of Letty Ogleton and her family demonstrates that enslaved people used their kinship ties to challenge the notion of black people as property. In September 1810, Ogleton and her five children—Henry, Michael, Lucy, Lucky and Charles—filed a petition of freedom with the Prince George's County Court. According to the petition, the members of this family were "entitled to their freedom having lineally descended from a free woman."[2] Ogleton was part of a complex familial circle that included individuals scattered across Prince George's County. Between 1810 and 1811, eight petitions were filed on behalf of twenty-one people, though all but one case were dismissed.[3] One petitioner, Sarah Ogleton, did not appear in court.[4]

Though most members of the Ogleton family did not win their petitions for freedom, their narrative is no less important. Much like the Boston family, whose freedom suits Schweninger has recently examined, the Ogletons offer a window into the crucial narratives of freedom both constructed and maintained by families of African descent in Maryland.[5] Unlike the Bostons, however, we have very little archival evidence about the particulars of the Ogletons claims. Despite the fact that they were enslaved by seven different owners and lived a distance from one another, all of the Ogletons advanced the same claim: they were descended from Maria Ogleton, "a free East Indian woman[,] in the maternal line."[6] Thus, petitions such as those advanced by the Ogletons also reveal how freedom is rooted in reproduction and how the black woman's body constructed slavery and freedom in the late eighteenth century.

Freedom petitions reveal the complexities of race and gender in an age marked by revolution. According to the testimony of her descendants, Maria Ogleton did not look "black." Rather, she resembled indigenous people, with flowing black hair and red skin. Her progeny argued that her origins were rooted, at least in part, among the Eastern Caribbean Arawaks. This argument constituted a strategic navigation of the racial landscape. Maryland's more celebrated freedom cases reveal that manumission was more likely to be granted if one could cite a white, Indian, or non-American black woman as one's mother.[7] If proximity to whiteness aided a freedom suit, then it is also equally fair to assume that a distancing from "blackness"—perhaps more concretely, a distancing from what would later be considered "African American"—also aided those seeking freedom.[8] As in this case, petitions delineated the intersections of race, gender, reproduction, and motherhood and how they manifested in black women's lives and those of their descendants. "Blackness" was malleable, whereas biology was not. In the eyes of the court, blackness remained synonymous with slavery, yet notions of the black woman's body as evidence and as spectacle replayed themselves throughout Maryland court records.

Slaveholders often paid little attention to the biological connections among the people they owned, however, the same could not be said of the enslaved. Testimony grounded in African American oral culture demonstrates that enslaved people not only recounted the lives of their forbears but also used that knowledge as grounds for their emancipation.[9] In this way, enslaved women in Maryland shared similarities with African American women who petitioned for freedom in revolutionary-era New England. Catherine Adams and Elizabeth H. Pleck, for example, demonstrate that the African American women's struggles in New England courtrooms constituted an extension of family members' efforts to live together and secure freedom for those still in bondage.[10] In the decades following the American Revolution, the Ogletons and others hoped that by tracing their lineage to a free woman, they could circumvent a life in bondage.

The Ogletons likely were dismayed at losing their suits but continued to labor for their owners. Their example reveals much about how enslaved people made the transition from property to self-possession not just in the United States but also in other areas of the African diaspora. Alejandro de la Fuente suggests that some enslaved people in Cuba expressed social agency by making claims on the legal system.[11] Similarly, Laura F. Edwards argues that enslaved women's actions and reactions to enslavement shaped South Carolina law.[12] Camillia Cowling maintains that enslaved women's deployment of motherhood rights helped define freedom in Spanish slave societies.[13] Enslaved women in Maryland, including Letty Ogleton, entered the court record as litigants petitioning for their freedom or that of their children. Such cases raised questions regarding the woman's complexion, hair, and physical features. Indeed, both in Maryland and beyond, from the late eighteenth century to the middle of the nineteenth century, black women's bodies held the potential to determine their claims to freedom.

Freedom and Black Women's Positionality during the Age of Revolution

African Americans' quest for freedom was not just mapped on the black woman's body; where they traveled often determined whether they or their descendants had a claim to freedom. Maryland's position (and in particular that of Baltimore and Annapolis) on the Atlantic littoral meant that black women's bodies and the spaces they inhabited and visited also held implications for freedom.

Enslaved Africans and African Americans in the newly formed United States borrowed the language of the American Revolution to advance their claims to freedom. In New England, for example, Elizabeth Freeman, a midwife and domestic, became the first African American to petition for her freedom in what became the United States. Known as "Mum Bett," Freeman (and many other free blacks of the era) shed the name bestowed by her owners and took the name "Freeman" to signify her new status.

Other revolutionary-era blacks used the courts to test the limits of their freedom. In 1781, New England resident Quok Walker became the property of a man named Jennison when he married Isabell Caldwell. Caldwell had promised Walker his freedom but reneged when she remarried. Walker eventually ran away, but Jennison and other whites found him and beat him severely. Because Walker believed freedom to be his natural right, he did not feel the need to sue for it; rather, he sued Jennison for assault. Douglas Egerton suggests that Walker and other "black Americans immediately expected the Revolution to offer not merely new opportunities for freedom but also full participation in the new political order."[14] Thus, the courts provided a place for African Americans to sue for freedom.[15]

The process for petitioning for freedom was long and expensive. Bringing freedom suits in Maryland, as in other places in the United States, meant that the enslaved possessed enough social capital for someone to believe their case was worth advancing. Many plaintiffs benefited from their relationship with Quakers or members of other antislavery religions or organizations, who would file suits on behalf of those seeking freedom. Schweninger notes that fines and court costs could run to hundreds or even thousands of dollars.[16] That enslaved people devoted what little money they had to such efforts indicates the value they placed on freedom. Lawyers filed suits as well as motions to ensure that plaintiffs and defendants appeared in court. The Ogletons' lawyer, Enoch Lowe, for example, followed their freedom petitions with summonses to the Ogletons' various owners. Moreover, Lowe also filed a motion forbidding the owners from selling or removing the Ogletons out of the state. Suing for freedom, then, involved a complicated, long, and expensive process that held the potential for danger.

Enslaved Africans who brought freedom suits weighed the consequences of their actions. When Jean Baptiste, an émigré from Saint-Domingue to Baltimore, filed a freedom petition in 1818, he faced violent retaliation in his owner's home.[17] According to Schweninger, "the court usually made arrangements for the protection of the plaintiff during the period of litigation. If they were returned to their owners the court often required the owner to post a bond; if they feared retribution, the plaintiffs could be turned over to the sheriff for protection and hired out for payment of fees; very few ran away; [very few] were severely punished for bringing suit. Some slaves suing for freedom asked for injunctions prohibiting owners or others (slave traders) from taking them beyond the court's jurisdiction."[18] Some of these cases were appealed and went on for years, with the plaintiffs working as hirelings under court supervision.[19] In some cases, the courts enjoined owners from selling petitioners while their cases were being heard. In other instances, the courts stipulated that owners could be punished if the slaves were harmed. And in still other cases, the courts assumed legal responsibility for the enslaved.[20] Nevertheless, enslaved people did not fully trust the law to protect them. After all, the law kept them enslaved. Enslaved people weighed the risks and filed suits anyway.

Freedom petitions highlighted the tensions involved when pieces of "property" sued for personhood rights. Ira Berlin suggests that in the decade following the American Revolution, state legislatures were "flooded" with freedom petitions.[21] From 1780 to 1789, for example, the Maryland General Court of the Western Shore (the state's highest court and the only place to bring a freedom suit at that time), heard just eleven petitions from enslaved people (though some of those petitions included multiple plaintiffs).[22] The power of the petitions thus lay not in their number but in what they represented. Petitioners consistently sought freedom despite laws designed to keep them in bondage, in the process demonstrating solidarity with those filing suits in other states. And while eleven seems like a small number, it far exceeds the totals for other states during the same period: in Virginia, for example, higher-level courts heard three such cases between 1780 and 1789.[23] Bringing cases to the highest court in either state was certainly not an easy task. Cases sometimes lasted years and did not always result in freedom.

African Americans' relationship with the law had fluctuated prior to the revolution. A 1664 directive provided that the child of a white woman and a black man (slave or free) would be a slave. A 1681 measure repealed the earlier law but forbade blacks from testifying in court cases, though it did allow enslaved people to sue for their freedom on the grounds that they were descended from a white woman. For that reason, the majority of Maryland's freedom suits, including those by the Ogletons, did not invoke the language of the American Revolution, such as equality and liberty, but rather cited the white status of petitioners' mothers. When Eleanor Toogood sued Annapolis doctor Upton Scott, for example, she testified that she was descended from "a free white woman and well entitled to her freedom." From October 1782 to May 1783, the court heard Toogood's case, in which she presented evidence that she was the granddaughter of a white indentured woman "who served her time" and an East Indian black man identified only as Dick who was owned and later freed by Thomas Beale of St. Mary's. Toogood's mother, Ann Fisher, had previously petitioned for freedom, claiming that her parents had been "lawfully married by the priest of the Romish church." Even though her petition had failed, the court found that Toogood's claim was valid. Scott appealed, but Toogood remained free.[24] It is not clear why she succeeded where her mother had failed, especially because evidence of descent from a white woman was not ruled as admissible in court until 1786. Eleanor may have won her freedom because her story was well known around Annapolis or because Annapolis was the state capital, the city was rather small, and Scott was well known.

A 1787 petition changed access to freedom for Maryland's African Americans. Mary Butler, an enslaved washerwoman from St. Mary's County, was descended from an Irish immigrant, Eleanor Butler, and "Negro Charles," an enslaved man, who married in 1681. It is probably not a coincidence that they married the same year that the 1664 law regarding slavery was repealed. They had reason to believe that Eleanor would remain free and that their children would not face a life of servitude. However, Eleanor's children found themselves enslaved.[25]

Oral tradition was important to Eleanor and Charles's progeny, who were raised knowing their forbears' story. Mary Butler's father, William claimed that he was a grandson of Eleanor and Charles, while her mother, also named Mary, believed that she was a great-granddaughter.[26] Such marriages between cousins were common given the ways that slavery affected lineage.

In 1770, Mary's parents unsuccessfully petitioned for freedom. Seventeen years later, their daughter did likewise, but she won. T. Stephen Whitman suggests that Butler succeeded where her parents had not because of a lack of definitive evidence that Eleanor and Charles had married, meaning that her descendants could not be enslaved under any laws.[27] Martha Hodes, however, provides evidence that witnesses testified that a wedding had taken place.[28] The court ultimately ruled in Mary Butler's favor after listening to hearsay evidence that had previously been inadmissible but was now permitted in courts.[29]

Scholars agree that the admission of hearsay evidence changed the trajectory of freedom suits in Maryland.[30] The transformative power of hearsay evidence resonates in the cultural realm as well. The orality of African and African American cultures proved valuable when narrating a family's history. African Americans provided detailed testimonies documenting their family lines. And, as Schweninger shows, the majority of court testimonies demonstrate that women were charged with preserving the family genealogy through oral tradition.[31] Following the Butler ruling, members of several enslaved families in Maryland—including the Shorters, Browns, and Bostons as well as the Ogletons—filed petitions based on descent from a free white woman.[32]

The admission of hearsay evidence effectively allowed black women's words, actions, and bodies to be entered as evidence in court cases. When brothers Charles and Patrick Mahoney sued for their freedom in 1791, they relied on their ancestor's body and travels to advance their claims for freedom. The Mahoneys petitioned for their freedom from John Ashton, a high-ranking Catholic official and one of the founders of Georgetown University. The Mahoneys based their case on descent from Ann Joice, a free woman who was brought from Barbados to England sometime in the late 1670s and subsequently to Maryland. The Mahoneys' lawyers argued that because Joice had lived in England, neither she nor her descendants could be held as slaves, a claim based on good precedent. In 1772, Lord Mansfield of the English Court of the High Bench ruled in the case *James Somerset v. Charles Stewart* that slavery was "unsupported" in English common law. Further, Mansfield determined that it was unlawful to forcibly bring a slave into England. This case contributed to the abolition of slavery in England and the emancipation of bondpeople throughout the British Empire.[33]

The *Somerset* case's reverberations across the British Atlantic have been widely acknowledged, but its use by a Maryland plaintiff expands our understanding of its implications. As Eric Papenfuse notes, the Mahoneys' case drew Maryland into a larger transatlantic debate about lineage, liberty, and the abolition of the slave trade.[34] The use of *Somerset* certainly signals that Maryland's legal culture was in step with the rest of the Atlantic world and that the Mahoneys understood the implications of their ancestor's time in England. In 1798, the court granted Charles his freedom, though the ruling was reversed on appeal. Charles and Patrick Mahoney ran away but were caught and returned to Ashton.[35]

Despite their defeat in court, the Mahoneys received their freedom from Ashton in 1804 when he moved to Cecil County. The following year, Ashton freed one of their siblings, Daniel. By 1808, at least six of the seven Ashton brothers had been freed either by Ashton or by fellow Catholic Charles Carroll of Carrollton. After a decade of legal wrangling, Ashton (and Carroll) may have concluded that the Mahoneys would not be deterred in their legal and extralegal attempts to gain freedom and that the effort required to keep them enslaved was not worth it. Another slave, Edward Queen, also sued Ashton for freedom in 1791, citing assault and battery by his owner as well as descent from a free black woman. The court agreed that Queen had been falsely enslaved and in 1795 granted him his freedom. Following the ruling, twelve more members of the Queen family ran away from Ashton, and he eventually granted ten of them their freedom.[36] The Queens and the Mahoneys were consuming considerable amounts of Ashton's time. Ashton's practice of owning slaves also came under fire from other Jesuits, criticism that may also have influenced his decision to let these bondpeople go.

The Mahoneys and the Queens exemplify how the Haitian Revolution influenced Maryland's legal culture.[37] As French slave owners fled the island of Saint-Domingue with their human chattel, they produced waves of retaliatory rulings by American and West Indian courts. According to Papenfuse, the rebellion in Saint-Domingue influenced the court's decision to deny the Mahoneys their freedom.[38] Indeed, those events triggered responses from whites and blacks throughout the Atlantic.[39] For whites, the uprising represented the culmination of their worst fears, with previously loyal slaves picking up machetes and attacking their masters.[40] For blacks, in contrast, the Haitian Revolution outlined a world of new possibilities. Haiti connected slaveholders and the enslaved to a larger circle of rebellion in the Atlantic world. Rather than an isolated incident, the events in Haiti represented a new social order.

Haiti also represented a complicated relationship among property, power, and place. White Marylanders welcomed slaveholders fleeing Saint-Domingue but were less happy about black émigrés. In 1792, lawmakers passed a measure requiring slaveholders from Saint-Domingue who resettled in the state to wait three years before releasing their slaves from bondage. The presence of blacks who might spread the contagion of rebellion clearly shaped the parameters of southern legal culture.[41]

In November 1797, Margaret Creek and her lawyer filed a petition in the Baltimore County Court, claiming that Creek "had been entitled to her freedom from birth" because she was "the daughter of Rachel who was the daughter of an Indian woman named Moll or Mary" who was "a free native of America who lived and died" as such. In March 1800, after three years in the court system, Creek, like the Mahoneys and the Queens, was declared free.[42] Though very little additional information is available about Creek, it is clear that she was sure of both her African and her Native American heritage. In this way, she resembles the enslaved women in Cuba who, as Cowling discusses, asserted their rights and thus reminded the court that they were not property. In Cowling's view, by making legal claims, black women forced the court and by extension lawmakers to view the enslaved as people and black women as women. Gendered values were assigned to freedom, but when black women entered the courtroom, they called into question the practices of law that placed them outside discussions of liberty, independence, and freedom.[43] This idea is particularly important when considering the differences between Creek, who embodied the complexities of race, gender, and status, and black women in Maryland whose bodies entered the court record as evidence.

Catherine Booth, for example, entered the court record via testimony presented when one of her descendants, Richard Booth, petitioned the Maryland General Court in 1792, claiming that he "was descended from a free woman and ... unjustly deprived of his Liberty by David Weems."[44] Booth maintained that his great-grandmother, Catherine Booth, had been freed by her owner, King Harrison.[45] Booth's petition was initially denied, and the results of his appeal are unknown. But the records of the appeal illustrate the ways in which physical appearance and racial logic were appended to freedom claims.

Scattered through some seventy pages of court testimony are the outlines of a second trial—that of Catherine Booth. Witnesses on both sides answered a series of questions: Were they related to either Weems or Richard Booth? Did they know Catherine Booth, her daughter, Sally; or Sally's daughter, Esther, who was Richard Booth's mother? What did they know about Catherine's status as free or slave? What did she look like? How did her hair look? Such questions were common in petitions based on descent from a free black woman. In this instance, witnesses gave conflicting accounts of Catherine's status, heritage, skin color, and hair texture.[46] As with the case of the Ann Joice, plaintiffs who could prove that their ancestors did not look black often had greater chances for freedom.

Black women's bodies were used as evidence; ironically, however, distance from blackness provided a loophole that enabled enslaved persons to win their cases. When black women's bodies entered the courtroom as evidence, they connected descendants to the revolutionary Atlantic in ways that are not always obvious. If a female ancestor were free, if she traveled someplace and her status changed, or if she lacked distinctly African traits, her descendants used these facts as a strategy for laying a claim to freedom. The quest for freedom thus caused some African Americans to renounce their racial identity (at least on paper). The nature of these court cases conveys the existence of something fundamentally unquantifiable and at the same time straightforward about the influence of black women on revolutionary society. Their presence constructed notions of freedom and independence as they served as a foil for revolutionaries who were white, male, and visible. For their descendants, black women's positionality was marked by geography, physicality, and physiology, and freedom was marked biologically.

Black Women as Wombs; Black Women as Agents; Black Women as Mothers

Petitioners in the late eighteenth century counted on genealogy to bolster their freedom claims. However, by the beginning of the nineteenth century, the courts responded by essentially cutting off genealogical claims to freedom even as they reinscribed the relationship between reproduction and racial slavery. Just after the turn of the century, county courts throughout Maryland were authorized to hear freedom suits. Enslaved men and women could present cases in local courts, thus avoiding the obstacles that prevented access to the state's higher courts, which could hear only appeals. Even more important, in November 1809, the Maryland legislature passed a measure that sought to prevent bondpeople from petitioning for freedom based on their mothers' status. The Act to Ascertain and Declare the Condition of Such Issue as May Hereafter Be Born of Negro or Mulatto Female Slaves enabled planters to determine the status of any living or future child born to bondwomen to whom they had promised freedom. If declarations of the status of future children were not made when the manumission document was presented in court, "then the state and condition of such issue shall be that of a slave."[47]

Presented a year after the U.S. Constitution had outlawed participation in the international slave trade, the 1809 law reconciled two opposing yet interrelated facts. First, the existence and expansion of the southern slave system depended on the reproductive labor of bondwomen.[48] Slave owners were keenly aware that enslaved women might conceive children after having been promised freedom but before being released from bondage. The decision to free an enslaved woman involved measuring the potential value of her future labor against the loss of the physical and reproductive labor of both mother and child. Indeed,

Whitman suggests that the majority of young girls who were promised freedom remained in slavery well past their childbearing years.[49] Second, the propensity of Maryland owners to manumit slaves had the potential to dismantle the slave state. By passing the 1809 law, legislators attempted to foreclose manumitted women's ability to produce free offspring by closing avenues to freedom based on the mother's status. In doing so, legislators, many of whom owned bondpeople, reaffirmed slaveholders' ability to assert power over their property. Moreover, the 1809 law represented what lawmakers, slaveholders, and bondpeople already knew: freedom, like enslavement, was tied to a bondwoman's womb.

By the time this measure passed, planters were aware that the only legal way they could obtain new slaves was through the reproductive work of their enslaved female population, increasing the already formidable economic incentives against manumission. The law's emphasis on the slave status of the children of manumitted women effectively mandated enslavement for another generation of African Americans and ensured that owners would continue to profit from enslaved labor.[50] The law followed the precedent set in New Amsterdam during the seventeenth century, whereby the enslaved received "half-freedom." In exchange for their freedom, enslaved men and women agreed that both their present and their future children would be enslaved and would work for the Dutch West India Company. As in New Amsterdam, gradual emancipation of children often meant that they remained under the control of their mother's master until they reached adulthood.[51] Owners thus retained control of children until either little profit resulted from their labor or they had reached an age of self-sufficiency. A substantial number of antebellum Baltimore's free blacks were born as slaves and gained their freedom as young or middle-aged adults.[52] Such practices may have arisen as a consequence of planters' reluctance to lose the potential revenue from sales of young children. If that was the case, then the 1809 law sought not to expand freedom through the manumission of bondwomen but rather, as Whitman argues, to constrict freedom by allowing planters to determine the status of slave children.[53]

Though the 1809 law restricted access to freedom for future generations, it did not diminish African American women and their descendants' efforts to use legal and extralegal measures to access freedom. In the ten years before the law was passed, six African Americans had filed freedom petitions in Maryland.[54] During 1810–20, ten did so.[55] From 1799 to 1809, Maryland county courts received twelve freedom petitions, a number that jumped to seventeen between 1810 and 1820.[56]

Petitioners had to prove that their status as enslaved, free, or gradually manumitted had been delineated prior to their mother's manumission. Such was the case of Lurena and her daughter, Ellen. In 1810, Rezin Hammond's last will and testament had promised Lurena freedom when she reached age thirty as well as freedom for all of her children when they reached age twenty-nine. Hammond's heirs failed to honor his wishes, not only keeping the two women in bondage but selling them in 1810. Two years later, Lurena gained her freedom on the grounds that she was thirty years old at the time of Hammond's death, while Ellen was awarded freedom because she was born after the date of her mother's promised emancipation and thus had been illegally enslaved from birth.[57] This case illustrates how the complicated legal process of manumission could stretch across generations.

The 1809 law had three significant implications regarding how the black woman's reproductive body was deployed within the law. First, since the law was framed entirely in terms of "women and their issue," the families of manumitted women were not understood to include children's fathers. This framing altered the definitions of household and family. Second, the terms of the law often staggered the dates of manumission for women and their children, meaning that responsibility for the child rearing often was distributed through the mother's extended kinship networks. Third, the first two factors caused a shift in legal responsibility that laid the foundation for future dialogues about gender, race, and poverty. African American women responded by drawing from the same support systems that had aided them in slavery.[58]

The 1809 law also enabled planters to keep the children of manumitted women in case the economy called for enslaved labor in the future. On the one hand, the law could provide an opportunity to escape the system of slavery. On the other hand, it could prolong the enslavement of children. Yet interventions by enslaved women and their children challenged the goal of guaranteeing the future of slavery through natural reproduction.

While earlier generations of African Americans served as pieces of evidence used by their descendants to obtain freedom, their progeny became litigants petitioning for the freedom of their children, both in Maryland and elsewhere in the United States. Following her emancipation in New York, Isabella Van Wagenen (later known as Sojourner Truth) sued Solomon Gedney for selling her son, Peter, to an Alabama man. Van Wagenen won, and Peter was returned to her.[59]

Working within the system meant that for good or bad, enslaved people were subject to the law. Nat Turner's rebellion in Southampton, Virginia, while a victory in the eyes of the enslaved, produced tighter restrictions on the lives of manumitted women and their kin. Many southern states, including Maryland, required emancipated African Americans to leave. Such laws imposed particular hardships on manumitted women whose children were enslaved, who faced a choice between reenslavement for failing to leave the state and losing their children. In 1833, newly freed Sophia Tydings petitioned the judges of the Anne

Arundel Orphans' Court for permission to stay in Maryland so that she could remain close to her husband, who was free, and her ten children, who were still enslaved. Tydings's request was based on her role as a mother: her petition noted that she "still had an infant at her breast." She was allowed to stay for another twelve months.[60] The court records do not indicate whether she subsequently obeyed the order to leave her children. The court's willingness to grant such requests revealed prevailing notions about biology and the health and care of slaveholders' property. Permitting Tydings to stay in the state and nurse her child benefited the person who owned that child's labor.

Tydings's vulnerability to the court indicates part of the larger systemic violence of enslavement—the absence of a private life even in freedom. When Robert Williams purchased his wife, Susannah, he did so with the intention of freeing her. In 1805, however, Robert Williams was "deprived of his understanding," and the court labeled him a "lunatic."[61] Susannah Williams petitioned to have herself and her children freed rather than sold to another owner. The fact that his enslaved property was also his family was beside the point. In 1806, the Maryland General Assembly passed a law providing that Susannah and her children would be freed in six months' time.[62] In this case, freedom required Susannah to make her husband's medical condition a matter of public record, depriving her of a private family sphere.

For the enslaved people who brought suits, the experience of freedom was just as important as the legality of it. In 1832, "Negro Joe" sued for his freedom on the grounds that Lavinia, his grandmother, and Dinah, his mother, lived "free and undisturbed in possession of their liberty and freedom." Witnesses testified that the two women "were going at large as free women living acting and passing [as free] in all respects" following the 1797 death of their owner, William Machubin. They remained in the "free and undisturbed possession of their liberty" until after the 1824 death of Machubin's widow, Elizabeth, who "never set up any claim to them." In 1832, Elizabeth Machubin's second husband, John M. Burke, inherited her property and laid claim to Joe and several relatives. The Anne Arundel County Court ruled in Joe's favor; Burke appealed the decision to the Court of Appeals for the Western Shore, which upheld the lower court's ruling. Joe traded the experience of freedom enjoyed by his female predecessors for a legal document stating what he already knew to be true—he was not property.[63]

Freedom as an experience was not lost on free or enslaved blacks. Writing about free black women in South Carolina, Amrita Myers notes that glimpsing and experiencing freedom were precursors to formal emancipation.[64] Negro Joe and others experienced freedom and were perceived by others as free before acquiring that legal status.

In other cases, freedom was granted only on the condition of exile. Betsey and John, an enslaved couple in Frederick County, Maryland, as well as "any issue of her body" received freedom via their owner's will in 1828—provided that they "leave the United States."[65] This stipulation undoubtedly was connected to the fact that many members of the Maryland elite were active in campaigns to resettle blacks in Liberia.[66] Thus, freedom had the potential to break up extended families. In this instance, where the family enjoyed freedom was as crucial to lawmakers as how they enjoyed that freedom was to the enslaved.

Place mattered in the lives of black women, affecting their ability to live freely. In Washington, D.C., Sally Henry, a free woman of color, petitioned the court to prevent an owner from selling her daughter outside of the District on the grounds that a higher court was considering her daughter's emancipation case.[67] Henry's request was granted, though the outcome of the higher court case is not known. Only when Dred Scott and his family filed suit in 1846 would U.S. courts decide the question of whether African Americans were people or property. For African Americans, the answer was simple; for the nation, however, the question, the answer, and resulting developments led the country to civil war.

Conclusion

Despite the small number of petitions presented in the wake of the American Revolution, black women's presence in Maryland courts shifted dramatically from the late eighteenth to the middle of the nineteenth century. During the revolutionary era, African Americans used descent from white women or free black women to justify freedom. After 1809, however, that strategy became less effective. But black women consistently entered the courts as litigants on behalf of their children, and their successes gave hope and encouragement to others who were enslaved. Charity Folks and most if not all other enslaved African American mothers desired freedom for their children but did not or could not enlist the courts in these efforts; instead, they negotiated privately on their children's behalf. Folks indeed petitioned and negotiated for her children's freedom, but she did so not in court but directly with her owners.

Access to freedom in Maryland reaffirmed the central role of women's reproductive labor. The ability to petition for freedom based on the mother's status reveals the centrality of black women's bodies in the law. Even when petitioners cited descent from a white or Indian woman, an implicit statement was made with regard to the law: blackness equated to enslavement, and a distancing from blackness equaled freedom. The descendants of white, Indian, and black women demonstrated that manumission was linked to women's reproductive capacities.

The nature of the right to petition changed and along with it black women's ability to use the law to their advantage. Rather than being dissected as evidence, they became plaintiffs, citing their role as mothers to enhance their legal rights. Though the nature of how black women used and were used in court changed between the late eighteenth and mid-nineteenth centuries, African Americans' efforts challenged the intent of slavery through natural reproduction by demonstrating that freedom was also inheritable. In the decades leading up to the Civil War, women labored for the survival of the family, legal personhood, and freedom, leading the way in the development of a free black society in Maryland. They worked to ensure that they, their children, and their future generations would enjoy a life outside bondage, and in so doing they accepted the challenges of freedom. As the next chapter explores, the success of many manumission schemes resulted from the strength of the family and social networks in freedom.

Charity Folks Bishop.
Courtesy Maryland State Archives, Annapolis.

Last will and testament of Charity Folks, 1828.
Courtesy Maryland State Archives, Annapolis.

First-floor dining room, John Ridout House, 120 Duke of Gloucester Street, Annapolis, Maryland.
Courtesy Library of Congress, Washington, D.C.

The Ridout row houses at 110, 112, and 114 Duke of Gloucester Street, June 1936.
Historic American Buildings Survey, E. H. Pickering, Photographer. Courtesy Library of Congress, Washington, D.C.

Headstone for Charity Folks Bishop, St. Anne's cemetery, Annapolis, Maryland, December 2009.

Photo courtesy of the author.

Folks/Bishop family plot, St. Anne's cemetery, Annapolis, Maryland, December 2009.

Photo courtesy of the author.

CHAPTER 3

Commodities and Kin
Gender and Family Networking for Freedom, 1780–1860

> But covet earnestly the best gifts: and yet show
> I unto you a more excellent way.
> —I Corinthians 12:31 (KJV)

Enslaved women and their descendants used creative legal strategies and whatever means they had to pursue freedom, thereby demonstrating the value they placed on freedom as well as their commitment to that ideal. According to Orlando Patterson, enslavement was a form of social death, and freedom (and by extension manumission) was life.[1] Patterson suggests that manumission was a gift rather than a right, a thesis that obscures more than it illuminates regarding Charity Folks and countless other enslaved women. Manumission involved a complicated negotiation between the enslaved and their enslavers.[2] Access to family played prominent roles in many dreams of freedom. Sydney Nathans's research on Mary Walker and Heather Andrea Williams's work on African Americans in the post-Reconstruction period shows that newly freed people desired to find their people.[3] Because enslaved women viewed manumission as a communal endeavor rather than an individual act, it held important ramifications for families. While manumission served as a family survival mechanism, it positioned free family members in paradoxical relationships with slavery, capitalism, and kin.

The communal vision of freedom for many of those enslaved in Maryland had its roots on Africa's Gold Coast (present-day Ghana), the birthplace of most Africans brought to Maryland between 1700 and 1750, though that population subsequently became more diverse.[4] The Akan people of the Gold Coast did not view enslavement as permanent or place the good of an individual over the good of the community. This community ethos survived the Middle Passage and creolization and eventually outlasted enslavement in the New World.[5] Though the idea of liberty had no direct corollary in Akan culture, it did possess a notion of freedom as a community endeavor that influenced Akan-descended peoples in Maryland.

What did this viewpoint mean in Charity Folks's life? She and other enslaved people possessed a deep knowledge of community and personal freedom. Whereas Charity was determined to influence her own liberation, it is clear that John Ridout's decision to manumit her evolved over time. In 1795, Mary Ridout noted in a letter to her mother, that her husband "did not approve of leaving [his slaves] to any person during their life.... He said Ruth and Charity had been two such faithful servants that he desired more might be done for them than the rest. That if I survived him he requested me if they were living to leave them a small annuity to maintain them comfortably ... all which I promised to comply."[6] In May 1797, John Ridout added two codicils to his will. In the first, he bequeathed to his wife, Mary, "my Negroes called Ruth, Hannah, Jack and Milly, also her trusty Mulatto Charity." In the second codicil, he awarded Folks her freedom in 1807. He also outlined his intention to free any of Charity's children still in bondage.[7] Thus, Ridout's gratitude converged with Charity's vision of freedom, even if liberation was delayed.

John Ridout died in 1797, and within two months, Mary Ridout signed a deed granting Folks immediate manumission. Mary Ridout also allowed Hannah and Lil' Charity to "stay with their mother," though time still remained on their terms of enslavement.[8] Mary Ridout also indicated her intention to grant James freedom in 1812, though he remained enslaved at a Ridout property some distance from Annapolis. In this case and many others, freedom and enslavement coexisted within the same family, posing a particular challenge for mothers.

African American women such as Charity Folks were well versed in the process of manumission. Indeed, the 1797 deed freeing Folks was only one marker in her and her family's longer struggle for freedom. At least five family members had preceded her in the transition from slavery to freedom. Her mother, Rachel Burke, had earned her freedom as an adult and later purchased the freedom of her son, Folks's brother, James.[9] In 1794, Charity's husband, Thomas Folks, bought his freedom from John Davidson.[10] John Ridout manumitted Charity's eldest daughter, Harriet Jackson, in 1786, when she was approximately five years old.[11] Five years later, Ridout freed Mary Folks, Charity's third eldest child, though Charity remained enslaved.[12] Rather than stay with their mother at the Ridout house, Charity's daughters lived with Rachel Burke and Thomas Folks.[13] Charity Folks was no doubt elated that her children had escaped the cruelties of human bondage but pained by their separation from her. When Folks was manumitted in 1797, her joy at having finally gained her own freedom must have been tempered by her fears for her children who remained enslaved and by the pain of separation from them. The path to freedom for African American families via manumission was narrow, rarely wide enough for more than two or three individuals to walk abreast.

The process of manumission reveals African Americans' complicated history with freedom. What does it mean when pieces of property engage in market transactions? What does it mean to purchase a family member as a commodity? Enslaved women in Maryland addressed these questions and others as they negotiated for their freedom and that of their kin. Most free persons had at least one relative or friend who had been enslaved or who remained in bondage.[14] African American women saw manumission as perhaps an attainable goal and relied on a community ethos while pressing for their own liberation and that of their family members. But freedom also had its price, and these women had no choice but to concede that the system won when they ran away, leaving their children behind, or when they acknowledged that they could not afford to buy their children's freedom.

African Antecedents:
Manumission, Property, and Community

Africans who lived along the Gold Coast possessed an entirely different viewpoint of slavery from the one that existed in the New World. Oral traditions passed down from those who survived the Middle Passage held that slavery was not an absolute—it was not permanent, it was not inherited, and in most cases, it was not perpetual. To the Akan peoples, slavery was a status, a consequence of actions or events, not the totality of a person. The enslaved were regarded as human beings who were entitled to certain rights and privileges.[15] In addition, Akan beliefs in the power of community prevented many manumitted women from divorcing themselves from the enslaved community. Individual manumission was seen as a stepping-stone to the liberation of an entire family. Whenever possible, members of Akan communities sought to bring others with them into the world of freedom.

By the eve of the American Revolution, the vast majority of Maryland's African Americans were one or two generations removed from Africa, with only remnants of the continent visible "in the appearance and intonations of their parents."[16] But the enslaved community maintained elements of African culture such as herbal knowledge, spiritual practices, and naming customs. Some cultural retentions were largely unseen by slaveholders but were nevertheless crucial to the sacred and secular lives of those enslaved. Bondpersons dreamed of and prayed for freedom, but the prayers and religious practices of the enslaved often remained secret from their owners.

Landownership and family constituted one of the Akan people's most important cultural markers and were reflected at several points in Charity Folks's life. Dylan Penningroth's analysis of property holding among both African Americans after Reconstruction and the Akan peoples of Ghana is particularly compelling, demonstrating the value African descendants placed on owning land and having access to their families.[17] Penningroth's research demonstrates that although property rights among post–Civil War African Americans and those in postemancipation societies in Ghana appear dissimilar, they have some commonalities—for example, the notion of property as both physical land and family lines.[18]

Labor, Hiring, and Power

The ability to participate in the economy influenced slaves' agency, in turn shaping the formation of slaves' families. Cultivating private farming plots not only provided bondpersons with additional food for their families but might enable them to barter or sell the surplus and thus acquire cash that could be used to purchase small material goods or eventually freedom. According to Damian Pargas, the enslaved "took advantage of various labor incentives to work for their own gain on Sundays and other holidays."[19] Pargas presents enslaved families as diverse in composition yet remarkably similar in their goals of freedom.

The variety of crops grown in Maryland ensured that many enslaved people hired themselves out and, if their owners allowed, used the time to try new experiences. Former slave William Cornish recalled that when he hired out, "I could go to Baltimore and stay a week or two, or go to a camp meeting. I would go and come back, so [the owner] had confidence in me, and didn't believe that I wanted to leave him." Eventually, Cornish "wouldn't go home only once in a while."[20] By having earned and by maintaining his owner's trust, Cornish used the situation to his advantage, gaining a measure of freedom and money.

However, being hired out could be traumatic for young children and very difficult for families. Elizabeth, who was enslaved in the late eighteenth century, felt lonely and isolated when she was hired out at eleven years old: "I thought I should die, if I did not see my mother." When the overseer denied her requests to see her family, she went home of her own accord. In response, the owner "tied me with a rope, and gave me some stripes of which I carried the marks for weeks."[21] Other former slaves shared Elizabeth's pain. Frederick Douglass recounted, "Frequently, before the child has reached its twelfth month, its mother is taken from it, and hired out on some farm a considerable distance off, and the child is placed under the care of an old woman, too old for field labor. For what this separation is done, I do not know, unless it be to hinder the development of the child's affection toward its mother, and to blunt and destroy the natural affection of the mother for the child."[22] Ultimately, whether the enslaved protested their separation from kin or came to accept it, hiring out broke up families, separated parents from children, and reminded bondmen and bondwomen that they were property.[23]

Indeed, hiring out could also cost the enslaved what they most wanted to preserve—their families. Dinah, who lived in Alexandria, Virginia, was hired out to her owner's kin in Baltimore County. One day, as Dinah was washing her clothes in a spring near the edge of the plantation, Martha Smith, one of the women in the home, ordered Dinah back to work. She responded that she "would come when it suited her" and doused Smith with water until she "lost her breath, fell to the ground and nearly drowned."[24]

While Smith returned to the house in search of dry clothes, Dinah attempted to run away to avoid punishment. Smith caught her, but Dinah threw the white woman to the ground. When Smith's husband returned and tried to punish the slave, Dinah responded by "kicking several times at his legs 'til they were so sore he could scarcely walk." She also scratched his hands severely, "promised to ruin him," threatened the life of one another family member, vowed to burn down the family's home, and verbally abused Martha Smith's sister, Sally Griffith.[25]

Griffith wrote to Dinah's owner, "I am afraid your Negroes will behave very bad. Dinah's example is too bad to go unpunished." It is not clear what sort of punishment Dinah faced or whether she received it, but she did manage to escape from the plantation, leaving behind her children.[26] Thus, exerting power over her own life had costs as well as benefits.

Power manifested itself differently in the lives of trusted servants and hirelings, whose travels could expand their social and familial circles. Leaving their places of residence enabled bondpeople to meet freeborn and manumitted blacks, thereby expanding informational networks as well as participating in the market economy. Charity Folks purchased lace, ribbon, silk, and wine on credit as needed for the Ridout home.[27] Store owner John Davidson noted that other enslaved people such as "the Mayor's Jemy," "Carrollton Carroll's Jack," "Dulany's Jack," and "Worthington's Sam" established credit on behalf of their owners.[28] Charity Folks's mobility expanded her world well before she was promised freedom. Being trusted enough to conduct market transactions enhanced a bondsperson's sense of personal power.

The ability to participate in market transactions resulted in moments of freedom. With money earned as market women, from trading goods grown in their gardens, from hiring out, and in some cases by doing overwork in the forges and furnaces, some fortunate enslaved women purchased freedom for themselves and their kin. In addition, they pushed the boundaries of bondage, challenging slaveholders' vision of bondpeople as mere commodities.

Enslaved Families: Purchasing Property, Manumitting Kin

Enslaved women channeled the community ethos present in West African society and meshed it with market transactions. In doing so they saw manumission as one step in the process of reuniting their families. Yet purchasing kin presented African American women with a paradox. By participating in these monetary transactions, they reinforced the idea of human beings as commodities. Sean Condon argues that group manumissions in Anne Arundel County not only show the ability of some African Americans to rescue multiple loved ones from bondage but also serve as a reminder of the limits facing other Maryland slaves who sought to acquire their legal freedom.[29] From 1780 to 1830, sixty-eight Anne Arundel deeds freed between six and nine slaves each, twenty-two deeds freed between ten and nineteen slaves each, and fifteen deeds freed twenty or more slaves.[30] The individuals named in these manumissions tended to be children, and they spent an average of at least ten more years enslaved after the documents were filed.[31] Such children were often too young to be hired out and possessed few marketable—and thus profitable from the owner's point of view—skills. However, owners were reluctant to free children, counting on the revenue they would generate as they grew to adulthood.

Enslaved women in Maryland bought their freedom or that of family members for as little as a shilling or five dollars and for as much as three hundred dollars. The smaller amounts carried primarily symbolic value and represented due diligence in transactions. In some Spanish colonies, for example, the custom of coartación required monetary compensation in exchange for legal freedom.[32] In Maryland, freedom could be purchased for one dollar, with the involvement of currency making the transfer of property legal. Larger amounts, however, clearly indicate the value a slave owner placed on the labor of the enslaved person.[33] Despite the legal aspect of the transition to freedom, Jennifer Hull Dorsey notes that for the most part, manumission remained a private affair between the enslaved and the slaver.[34] Some slaves were released with a pension, which in many cases they used to purchase their kin. For example, when Susanna Hawkins and her husband were freed, their owner gave them some money, which Susanna used to buy her daughter's freedom for twenty pounds.[35] In other cases, families negotiated agreements with slaveholders that allowed for reunification without freedom. Such linked transactions demonstrated the communal nature of freedom and highlight the complicated paths to manumission and purchase.

The ability to purchase one's own freedom or the freedom of a family member often depended on the presence of white allies. Calvin Schermerhorn suggests that Maryland slaves' ability to network offered them access to important information.[36] Specifically, enslaved people knew whether purchasing freedom was possible based on whether the owner was known to manumit the enslaved. For example, when large slaveholding families such as the Ridouts and Snowdens manumitted people, they often freed members of the same family.[37] For example, Mary Callahan freed Rachel and Lucy on December 24, 1801, in exchange for one hundred dollars.[38] In 1820, Callahan promised gradual freedom to three siblings, William (approximately age eighteen) in 1823 and Horace and Rebecca (both approximately age twelve) in 1829.[39] The siblings were the children of an Irish immigrant to Annapolis, William "Daddy" Bishop, and Jane Minsky, an enslaved woman owned by Callahan. Descendants suggest that Daddy Bishop purchased his wife and later freed her.[40] William Bishop and Jane were not satisfied with the gradual manumission of their children. In 1822, Callahan freed Rebecca and William Green freed Bishop after purchasing him from Callahan.[41] Bishop must have purchased Horace: a manumission document indicates that he freed his son in 1821.[42] The members of the Bishop family maintained their ties and formulated and executed a plan to achieve freedom.

Fewer than 5 percent of the 765 women manumitted in Anne Arundel County between 1780 and 1840 purchased their own freedom. Among them were Abigail, who bought her freedom for one hundred dollars after her owner's death in 1817, and thirty-seven-year-old Fanny, who paid forty dollars for her freedom the following year.[43] The low number of such transactions may stem in part from a failure to record them and in part from the fact that enslaved women had fewer chances to earn income than enslaved men. And in many instances, women gained their freedom when their husbands or other family members purchased it for them.

Whereas the number of women who purchased their own freedom was low in the first few decades of the nineteenth century, significant numbers of manumitted women purchased the freedom of their children. In 1812, Cassandra Johnson paid five dollars for her freedom and that of her three children, Milly, Evey, and Betsey.[44] In 1817 Susanna Mullin paid twenty dollars to purchase herself and her three children from bondage. Mullin's manumission document indicates that Richard Mullin purchased Susanna and her children from James Deale, but it does not disclose the relationship between Susanna and Richard.[45] In 1822, Hester Hood and Elizabeth Hood freed eight women and their twenty-nine children in exchange for fifty dollars.[46] In 1816, forty-year-old Fanny purchased freedom for herself and her son, William, for five dollars, with owner Araminta Harrison noting Fanny's ability to take care of William.[47] In other instances, owners asked much higher prices for their enslaved property: Eliza Hood demanded and received three hundred dollars from Kitty Prout in exchange for manumitting the woman and her son.[48] Such transactions signaled not only the enslaved person's value to the owner but also the value that the enslaved person placed on freedom.

When black women could not secure the immediate release of their children from bondage, they settled for gradual emancipation. On January 1, 1811, for example, Patty Lee gained her freedom from Horatio Samuel Gibson.[49] Over the next month, Lee bought her two children from Gibson, paying twenty dollars for the release of her six-month-old infant, Henry, when he reached the age of twelve. Lee then paid sixty dollars to secure freedom for her then three-year-old daughter, Anne, twenty years later.[50] In 1830, another woman, Juliet, purchased freedom for herself and her three children, though her children were to remain enslaved but in her care until they were older.[51] Casey Ellen, who was five years old, and Jane, who was four, were to serve their mother until they reached sixteen, while their brother, William, would not gain his freedom until he was twenty-one.[52] In this case as in others, laws that prohibited the freedom of children, required the labor of enslaved children to be entailed to their parents.

Enslaved women lobbied for their children's manumission when purchasing it was not an option. In 1800, James Henry of Baltimore County purchased Isabella on a twelve-year term slavery agreement. Two years later, Isabella gave birth to William; shortly thereafter, Henry freed the infant for less than one dollar at the "request of mother Isabella and grandmother," though his reasons for doing so are not clear.[53]

Black men, like black women, frequently attempted to purchase their kinfolk. Benjamin Badger, a free man of color in Anne Arundel County, freed his "yellow woman" in exchange for five dollars. Badger's relationship to this woman is unknown, but he may well have purchased the woman with the sole intention of freeing her, and she may have been his wife.[54] In 1816, John Adams, a free man of color, purchased Rachel and her child, Evina, from Mary Gassamay.[55] Two years later, Adams freed Rachel and Evina as well as a newborn baby, John. Adams likely purchased his family with the intention of freeing them later.

Free black men also purchased and then freed their wives and children after a period of term slavery. In 1801, George Johnson bought his wife, Mary, and her son from an Anne Arundel County slaveholder; eleven years later, he freed both of them as well as their daughter, Anna, who had been born in the interim, liberating his family from all forms of servitude to him or to his executors.[56] The reasons for the delay are not clear, but it may have been a condition of the agreement under which Johnson purchased his wife and her son.

Such sales allowed African Americans to reunite members of families scattered among multiple households. In separate June 1817 transactions, Philip Howard bought his wife, Maria Howard, from Isaac Paul, and his two children, George and Ruth, from Vachel and Paul Brown, paying one dollar for each of his family members. A year later, he issued gradual manumission deeds for his children, who were freed in 1823, when they reached the age of twenty-four. Also in 1818, he purchased Mary Ann, also listed as Philip's wife, from the Browns, paying one hundred dollars for her. Mary Ann, like Maria, was listed as Howard's wife.[57] It is possible that both documents referred to the same woman and that they returned to court to confirm her manumission after her free status was challenged. It is also possible that Maria Howard had died and her widower had remarried. Given the complicated family ties of the enslaved this particular path to freedom leaves this query unanswered.

Some attempts to purchase family members required additional arbitration and negotiation. Free black Perry Wright agreed to buy his wife and daughter from Charles Pettibone and paid him "the certain sum of money." However, Pettibone died before freeing the members of Wright's family. Horatio Ridout, a lawyer, intervened on their behalf and purchased the woman and child. He then returned to court to present Pettibone's will, which documented that Wright had paid his debt in full, before allowing Wright to purchase his family for a nominal fee.[58]

Relationships between black men and black women were not necessarily completely consensual, just as relationships between white men and black women exclusively centered on violence. It is impossible to gauge the dynamics of any husband-and-wife relationship, let alone one in which one of the parties was free and the other was enslaved. However, by purchasing their wives, black men asserted that their rights as head of households were on the same level as the rights of white men. But it does not follow that white men viewed black men as equals.

In some instances, white men married and then freed enslaved women. In 1780, planter William Reynolds purchased bondwoman Elizabeth and her two children from merchant and political leader Daniel St. Thomas Jenifer for ninety pounds. Reynolds then "intermarried" with Elizabeth, fathering two more of her children. During the late eighteenth and early nineteenth century, intermarried referred to marriages involving people of different races, ethnicities, statuses, or religions, among other factors. The term was not precisely the same as interracial marriage, nor did it by definition mean that one person was free and the other was enslaved, though such was indeed true in this case. In 1804, Reynolds freed his wife and two of her daughters, Nancy and Rachel.[59] Reynolds also freed John and Alexander, his sons with Elizabeth, and Abraham, Rachel's son. This case has a variety of intriguing features. The 1800 census lists Reynolds as the white head of a household that included four free blacks, yet the manumission deeds were not presented in court until 1804. In addition, all of the "children" freed were over the age of twenty when the documents were presented in court. Finally, this white man purchased children who were not his biological offspring.

Freedom via manumissions, like freedom via petition, could occur in a multitude of ways and could stretched over many years and great distances. Purchasers, like petitioners, stood a better chance of success if they were known in the community. In 1829, Samuel Snowden, a free black living in the Georgetown neighborhood of the District of Columbia, purchased his wife, Viney, from Anne Arundel's Thomas Snowden (likely Samuel's former owner). Samuel Snowden also purchased his three children, aged between four months and thirteen years, under a term slavery agreement—the girls until they reached sixteen and the boy until he turned twenty-one. At the end of the children's enslavement, Samuel was required to apprentice them or give them a trade so that "they would not become wards of the Orphan's Court of D.C."[60] The children also were forbidden to leave the District of Columbia, a difficult provision to enforce in light of the fact that the Anne Arundel Court was thirty miles away in Annapolis. This stipulation probably reflected Maryland laws that required the removal of former slaves from the state within a year of their manumission.

Purchasing family members was a lengthy and expensive process for free blacks, as Caroline Hammond discovered firsthand. Her father, George Berry, a free black, had married her enslaved mother with the consent of her owner, Thomas Davidson, who had agreed to let Berry purchase his wife within three years. According to Hammond, "Father paid Mr. Davidson for mother on the partial payment plan. He had paid up all but $40.00 on mother's account, when by accident Mr. Davidson was shot while duck hunting." Davidson's widow then raised the price to $750. In response, Berry and some friends planned and executed the escape of his wife and children to Baltimore.[61] Sometimes, families had no option other than fleeing.

Earning a wage provided free black women with the means to purchase family members and populate their communities with kinfolks. In so doing, these women found themselves in the precarious position of asserting enslaved personhood by buying someone else's property. Nonetheless their participation in these transactions demonstrated that they were shrewd networkers and negotiators. In Charity Folks's Maryland, the communal worldview of enslaved people existed alongside the liberalism bred by the American Revolution. For enslaved people, family figured prominently in conceptions of liberty, whereas slaveholders saw enslaved families as tied to the conception of property.

Condon suggests that large-group manumission accounted for nearly four-fifths of the several thousands of slaves freed between 1780 and 1830. Moreover, Condon suggests that persons who had free black relatives were more likely to be manumitted.[62] Although actions by free and enslaved black people pressed against the lines of slavery, manumission complicated family ties as much as it strengthened them.

The family unit, whether fractured or intact, remained important to African Americans, who developed competing notions of property as they tried to reclaim their kin. Although Perry Lewis's father, who had been born on Kent Island, was a free black, his mother was enslaved. Lewis later recalled, "The mother was the owner of the children that she brought into the world. Mother being a slave, made me a slave."[63] With this statement, Lewis clearly articulated the principle of the 1662 Virginia law that made enslaved children the property of the mother and unknowingly inverted the notion of partus sequitur ventrem (the status of the child follows that of the mother).[64] His words express what was common knowledge among slaves: mothers had the best (and perhaps only) chance of keeping their children with them, while fathers were often separated from their children. Likewise, enslaved women who lost their children to sale might have agreed with Lewis's assessment since they were powerless to prevent such sales.

Pro-slavery texts sought to perpetuate the notion that some African Americans found the idea of freedom unfamiliar and scary. Sarah Levering, for example, noted that a recently manumitted woman named Charlotte looked back at enslavement with "infinite longing and desired to return to her bonds." According to Levering, Charlotte so detested life as a free person that "it was agreed upon during my parents' lifetime, the children of these free parents remained slaves."[65] Not all enslaved persons were so adverse to freedom. When the Leverings moved from Baltimore to Ellicott City, Maryland, Margaret Jane Blake purchased her freedom.[66] It is of course quite plausible that Blake heard the story of Charlotte from a slaveholder who wanted to dissuade her from seeking her freedom: most enslaved families saw freedom as a welcome possibility rather than a source of fear. Rather than leaving their kin in bondage, newly manumitted women pooled all available resources to change the course of their children's lives, pulling African traditions into the New World.

Walking into Freedom with Charity's Folk

As a skilled caregiver, Folks must have known that Mary Ridout was terminally ill in 1807, and she might well have prodded the ailing woman to honor John Ridout's intention to free Lil' Charity and James. Folks knew enough about the law to make certain that the details of her freedom were not only spelled out but also executed. When Mary Ridout returned to court in 1807, she was accompanied by her older son, Samuel, the immediate past mayor of Annapolis, and her younger son, Horatio, a powerful lawyer and official in the Anne Arundel County Court. Leaving nothing to chance, Folks paid Ridout one dollar to execute the manumission document, which immediately released James and Lil' Charity and provided gradual manumission for Folks's grandchildren. Ridout also affirmed the legal viability of the previous documents that had freed the elder Charity, Harriet, Mary, and Hannah.[67] In total, four decades passed between the manumission of Charity Folks's first child and that of her grandchildren.

Folks thus walked into freedom with one of the most tangible expressions of property in African society, her family.[68] According to the 1810 census, Charity and Thomas Folks and three of their children were living in the same house.[69] In time, all of her children married and began families of their own. For the most part, the Folks family appears to be a success story. But what of those kinfolk who could not be rescued and were lost to slavery? An in-depth view of manumission cannot recover the voices of those separated from their families as part of wedding dowries, hiring arrangements, western migration, or Baltimore's (and increasingly Maryland's) position in the domestic slave trade. Looking specifically at the Reconstruction period, Heather Andrea Williams cautions us to investigate the trauma involved in separation.[70] As this chapter shows, gendered and family networks were crucial for slaves to purchase their freedom, which, in turn, allowed African Americans to reestablish their families within their own households. The next chapter focuses on how African American women maintained their free status and their families and recovered their power in the context of increasingly harsh legislation designed to limit that status, sever the ties that bound those families, and circumscribe that power.

CHAPTER 4

Moving Slavery, Shaping Freedom
Households and the Gendering of Poverty in the Nineteenth Century

> Out of the spoils won in battles did they dedicate
> to maintain the house of the Lord.
> —I Chronicles 26:27 (KJV)

Manumitted women fortified their family networks in freedom and pushed against slavery by competing in and sometimes thriving in a free wage economy. Drawing on Marylyn C. Wesley's notion that the endpoint of freedom is to be realized in a new location, this chapter focuses on the space of the household.[1] Freedom, like the composition of free black households, was multifaceted, including multiple generations of the same family. Despite class standing, laws aimed at controlling the free black population cut across economic lines, thereby complicating the already tenuous relationships among black women, their families, and the law. After 1807, Charity Folks and her children established their lives in freedom, but some of her grandchildren—three children of Harriet Jackson Calder—remained enslaved: five-year-old James until in 1818, three-year-old Ann until 1819, and infant William until 1822.[2] Such arrangements were not exceptional: Charity Folks, Thomas Folks, and Harriet Jackson Calder had all followed a similar path to freedom. What was exceptional, however, was that owner Mary Ridout allowed the children to live with Harriet and her husband, William Calder—that is, they had guardianship rights over their children until the term of enslavement expired. In exchange, Harriet agreed to "feed, clothe, support and maintain her said children." Harriet Calder was not only responsible for her children but was bound by law to either hire them out or have them trained as apprentices if she could not provide for them.[3] Provisions for the care and maintenance of freed children typically were put in place at manumission, yet in this instance, the maintenance for the enslaved children shifted from the slave owner to the free black mother. Planters' emphasis on enslaved women's offspring produced an environment that rendered African American women's parental responsibilities distinct from those of the men who fathered their children. This singular notion of parenthood followed African American women from slavery, through manumission, and into narratives about freedom. As Frederick Douglass intimated in his memoirs, the families of manumitted women were not understood to include the fathers of the children.[4] As a result, hereditary racial slavery, freedom, and notions of social responsibility became intertwined in the early nineteenth century. Consequently, this framing altered the legal definitions of household and family for manumitted women.

The Folks family also demonstrates that freedom was multigenerational and that freedom included black women's right to share a roof with their families. At times, the Folks household included not only Charity Folks's mother, Rachel Burke, but also some of Charity's grandchildren and great-grandchildren. Households functioned as the chief site of social organization in the South.[5] At a time when traditional notions of households were reserved for white male property owners, black women not only established independent households but did so against all odds. Free black households took a range of forms, incorporating people of various social and economic backgrounds. Focusing on households allows us to see black men despite their disappearance from most narratives of black families, and the ability to choose a partner and legally marry became one of the most central features of freedom.

The household was the site of multifaceted experiences of freedom. In keeping with Amrita Myers's suggestion, Charity Folks, her children, and her grandchildren demonstrate that freedom was experienced.[6] Enslaved families benefited from manumission, but the distance from enslavement was measured by degrees.[7] The legacies of slavery remained present in manumitted women's daily lives, and freedom was less a static condition than an ongoing and uneven multigenerational process, even within a particular household. The experiences of Folks and her family mirror some if not all of these phenomena.

Much of the scholarship on free blacks focuses on the exceptional and critical few who amassed property. Though manumitted women comprised the highest majority of free black women, the number of free black property holders remained quite small during the first few decades of the nineteenth century.[8] Wilma King notes that African American women "headed households, and were desperately poor and worked long hours each week for meager wages."[9] Even wealthy or better-off African Americans faced legal disadvantages that deprived them of some of freedom's promises. For example, African American women had no recourse in the face of laws requiring that free black children be bound into apprenticeships. Thus, these women's private experiences of mothering were profoundly affected by public measures that reached into their homes.

The Folkses' manumission experience encapsulates some of the tensions inherent in the complicated legacy of the 1809 Maryland law that sought to limit the means by which African Americans could challenge their enslavement. Women manumitted in the early decades of the nineteenth century reconciled increased opportunities for their own freedom against legal moves to bind their children and grandchildren into slavery or apprenticeships. In both cases, black women struggled to control the rights to their children's labor and thus silence the persistent echoes of slavery. As Stephen Whitman notes, "The manumission story stresses the transition to freedom theme and the apprenticeship story that of continuation of slavery."[10] The nature of the law and its emphasis on women as caregivers also meant that black men were legally written out of the family and were replaced by a precarious mate—the state. Indeed, even as the number of free blacks in Maryland rose, women found that slavery shaped their freedom and ultimately that of their descendants.

The Shape of Free Black Households

The term *free black household* fails to capture the shifting dynamics within the walls of the domicile. Slave hirelings often rented rooms in free black households, partners bought their spouses, and enslaved children occasionally lived with their free black parents or other relatives.[11] For many free black women, the house also served as a workplace. According to Barbara Wallace, 227 free black women appeared in the 1831 Baltimore directory as washerwomen, while twenty-three women identified as laundresses. In total some 250 women (roughly 86.5 percent) of free black women worked within their homes doing laundry for others.[12] The household, then, did more than reflect the multiplicity of African American relationships; it provided a central location where family and fictive kin, public and private, work and leisure, and free and enslaved all converged.

In 1790, there were 832 free black heads of household in Maryland.[13] Jennifer Hull Dorsey notes that on Maryland's Eastern Shore, some families wanted to live close to family members still in bondage but remain in black neighborhoods.[14] African Americans in Anne Arundel and Baltimore Counties followed this pattern. In Annapolis, free blacks lived on Gate Street, which took its name from the fact that it was where the gates to the city stood. In Baltimore City, free blacks tended to live a distance from the place of their enslavement yet still within the city limits to be close to their kin.

Free black households did not function in isolation from the outside world, and the location of such households in towns as small as Annapolis often tethered African Americans to their enslaved past. The Folks family, for example, lived within blocks of the Davidson and Ridout residences. In Baltimore, former bondspersons established residences in black enclaves within the city limits such as Fells Point and Jones Falls.[15] That Annapolis was not more than a large town and Baltimore an expanding city meant little, as free black settlement followed similar patterns regardless of locale. Free blacks remained in familiar locales precisely because their elaborate kin networks included those who were still enslaved.[16]

The household may have served as the site of social organization, but the ability to legally marry crystallized one's life in freedom.[17] Manumitted men and women viewed marriage as a right and defined exactly what constituted a marriage. Some chose to legally marry in churches, while honored commitments made by jumping the broom as bondpeople.[18] According to Seth Rockman, these types of success stories masked challenges African Americans faced in establishing conjugal households.[19] Some enslaved persons had spouses who were free. In other cases, husbands and wives were separated because one spouse did live-in work for whites. In addition, some newly freed African Americans quickly divested themselves of mates acquired during slavery. Others were so traumatized by their experiences in slavery that they chose not to take partners. It is unclear whether Charity and Thomas Folks ever legally wed, but they certainly considered themselves married.

Charity and Thomas Folks's children married and quickly established their own households as well. Charity's eldest daughter, Harriet Jackson, married a white Annapolis resident, William Calder, and they lived with their three children on Cornhill Street, two blocks away from the Folkses' home.[20] Charity Folks's son, James Jackson, married and had four children, though his wife disappears from the household after the 1820 Census.[21] Thomas's son, Henry, married a woman named Jane and relocated to Baltimore, where he and his son, Thomas, made shoes and boots at their shop on Mulberry Street.[22] Not much is known about Hannah Folks. When she died in the early 1820s, she left her young daughter, Elizabeth, in Charity Folks's care. Mary Folks married twice, first to Phillip Norris, a free man, and later to Moses Lake, another free man who was a barber at the U.S. Naval Academy. According to court testimony given by family friend, Hannah Murray, motherhood was a point of contention between Mary and her sister, Lil' Charity. Mary never had children, while Charity had six, and Mary believed that Charity consequently received more of their mother's attention.[23] Other free black people had more difficulty finding mates than did the women in the Folks family. Baltimore had three black women in their teens, twenties, or thirties for every two black men.[24]

On Maryland's Eastern Shore, free African Americans moved their free family members into autonomous households.[25] Yet members of families continued to live and work in their employers' homes. In Baltimore and Philadelphia, black women's labor as domestic servants frequently confined them to their employers' households.[26] In 1790, half of Philadelphia's 1,897 free blacks—most of them women—lived and worked in white households.[27] The household signaled freedom even when some family members lived elsewhere. Fictive kin also lived with people with whom they were enslaved. In this way, a household functioned as a home, centering families and providing them with a central hub.

African American women did not head the majority of free black households. Rockman's research shows that in 1810, women headed only 30 percent of Baltimore's black households.[28] In Talbot County, by contrast, 60 percent of the free African American households in 1832 were headed by women and comprised six or more people.[29] Factors such as an African proclivity for matrilineal and matrifocal social structures; the character of chattel slavery, which promoted abroad marriage and extended kin networks; and developments in the legal arena contributed to a complex structure for free black households that has increasingly been labeled as a distinct feature of culture among peoples in the African diaspora. Matrifocal and matrilocal kinship ties forged in slavery often influenced free black households.[30] Children freed while their mothers remained in bondage often went to live with free grandmothers, aunts, and/or sisters.[31] Female-headed households also included fictive kin—people not related by blood who were nevertheless treated as family members.

The overemphasis on women as heads of households often obscures the role of black men by shrouding their presence in an either/or binary. Either Census takers listed a free black man as the head of a household, or he ceased to exist entirely in that historical record. In freedom as in slavery, black men participated in the lives of their families when they lived near enough to do so. That black men headed households is clear, though there are only a few examples of men who did so as single parents—often when the mother remained in bondage. One Anne Arundel County man, James Sparrow, for example, assumed responsibility for his recently freed children while his wife, Nelly, finished out the term of her enslavement. Nelly's owner, American Colonization Society founder Margaret Mercer, had manumitted the Sparrow children under the condition that James provide for his children and for any child born to Nelly while she was enslaved.[32]

Free black men were also active stepfathers to children of different unions.[33] Thomas Folks was an active stepfather to Charity Folks's son, James Jackson, and daughter, Harriet Jackson, and James and Thomas spoke often about various "matters concerning the family." According to James, Thomas "wished to divide his property carefully amongst his children," including James, even though the two men were not biologically related.[34]

Black men were also entrusted with the responsibility of serving as guardians of elderly kin. Eighty-year-old Sarah (who would otherwise have been too old to be manumitted) and her grandson, Benjamin, received their freedom on the condition that he take "care in feeding and clothing" her. To make sure Benjamin lived up to his end of the bargain, their owner, Randolph Latimer Brandt, appointed Walter Boswell of Charles County to "judge ... if he finds her neglected"; in that case, Benjamin would be reenslaved.[35] Whatever Brandt's motives, the stipulation essentially kept Benjamin in a state of quasi freedom, since it subjected him to surveillance and he could involuntarily be returned to bondage. In other cases, grandparents assumed guardianship of grandchildren. Such provisions were in keeping with African Americans' sense of responsibility for their family members. According to Dorsey, on Maryland's Eastern Shore, "manumitted parents raised their freeborn children with a keen awareness of their obligation to care for and support grandparents, parents and siblings."[36]

Some of Maryland's free blacks created their households not in the United States but in Liberia. In some cases, they were forced to cross the Atlantic under the auspices of the American Colonization Society and later the Maryland Colonization Society; in other instances, they chose to make the move because they believed that Liberia offered a more meaningful, secure, and lasting freedom. Two of Charity's grandsons, Nicholas and Horace Bishop, were among those who headed to Liberia. There, society was organized around the male-headed household, in keeping with the popular conception of a self-sufficient American man abroad. In a sense, for African American migrants, manhood was synonymous with full citizenship rights and the ability to care for one's household.

African American women accounted for about half of those who immigrated to Liberia under the auspices of the American Colonization Society, traveling with their families, kin groups, and neighbors or occasionally alone.[37] Colonization society agents discouraged single women from making the journey because their situations did not fit traditional notions of male heads of household. Such migrations were also dangerous as a consequence of disease and difficult because of the need to find sustainable crops. Migrating to Africa certainly severed the tie to slavery, but migrants still faced hardships in experiencing freedom.

African Americans were divided on the issue of colonization, which incorporated debates over racial identity and national allegiance, black empowerment, and general emancipation.[38] Writing at the time, journalist John Russwurm argued that enslaved blacks would never be emancipated unless the free population resettled in Africa, an argument echoed by others.[39] Many other blacks agreed that the members of the free population had only one choice: "to continue a life of base subordination, or to flee."[40] Proponents of this position maintained that there was "no other home for the man of color of republican principles than Africa."[41]

Anti-emigrationists, in contrast, made the case for African American advancement in the United States. African Methodist Episcopal Church founder Richard Allen vehemently disagreed with resettlement, lamenting, "Why would they send us into a far country to die? See the thousands of foreigners migrating to America every year: and if there ground sufficient for them to cultivate, and bread for them to eat: why would they wish to send the first tillers of the soil away?"[42] Likewise, abolitionist and journalist/pamphleteer David Walker suggested that although the labor of slaves made the United States "as much our country as it is yours," emigration advocates, black and white, were "resolved to assail us with every species of affliction that their ingenuity can invent.[43] Contemporary scholar John Saillant agrees: "The . . . effort to remove black Americans to Africa or the Caribbean flowed from this view of the black man as alien to the unifying likeness required in a republic."[44] Moreover, as Michelle Mitchell notes, black abolitionists conflated emigration and colonization to make the point that free blacks should not estrange themselves from those who remained in bondage; Liberia seemed especially tainted by its association with the American Colonization Society.[45]

Remaining in Maryland, for whatever reasons, left black households the site for contested meanings of freedom. Yet no matter the configuration, the household did not completely erase the enslaved experience. Although free blacks understood themselves to be free, the shadow of their enslaved past always loomed. Despite Charity Folks's desire to keep the members of her family close, their experiences in slavery continued to drive a wedge between them. Ironically, manumission produced feelings of resentment among Folks's children, and James Jackson, among others, thought that she "appeared to have a greater fondness" for Lil' Charity, who remained enslaved after the other children were freed and thus spent the most time with and wielded the greatest influence over her mother. According to Jackson, even Thomas Folks had remarked that Lil' Charity's influence "would carry his wife to hell."[46] For their part, Jackson and another daughter, Mary Folks, also believed that they had been unfairly separated from their mother when they were young, a viewpoint that reflected the lasting influence of slavery and that led to a long-standing rivalry between Mary and Lil' Charity.[47]

Charity's obvious preference for one child over another produced a long-standing rivalry between Mary and Lil' Charity. Their brother, James Jackson, believed that his mother's preference stemmed from "Mary being taken away from her mother when a small child."[48] The sibling rivalry caused the elder Charity "a good deal of trouble," and she feared that their hostility toward one another "would bring her grey hairs" and would persist even after she died.[49] The sisters competed for men as well as for their mother's loyalty, and as Charity had predicted, in 1835, after her death, they fought over eighteen inches of property separating their homes.[50] Mary and her husband, Moses Lake, sued Lil' Charity and her husband, William Bishop, for erecting a gate in the alley that prevented the Lakes from accessing their home.[51]

The tension in the family had been exacerbated when William and Charity Bishop moved into the Folks home on Church Circle. Lil' Charity reorganized the house and ordered her brother, James Jackson, to remove the hogs he kept in the yard. James removed the pigs, but a volatile argument ensued in which James drew "a knife on [his mother] and called her ill names." Charity Folks never forgave her son and removed him from her will, a significant penalty because she had amassed a considerable fortune.[52]

Charity Folks and her family demonstrate that among Maryland blacks in the early nineteenth century, the household served as a physical manifestation of a multifaceted freedom. Within its walls, black women married, cohabited, and raised children. Other black women lived away from their families in the white households, separated from their loved ones by wage labor. Though they were no longer enslaved, neither were they free to create homes solely in accordance with their desires.

Property, Economic Mobility, and Class Development

African American women also had a multiplicity of experiences in the free labor market. For the most part, manumitted women and the members of their households worked hard to survive. Some manumitted women received small allowances from their former owners, providing a bit of a cushion against financial hardship. In his will, John Ridout directed his heirs to care for Charity Folks and to pay her twelve Spanish silver dollars and other "aspects of his estate."[53] Ridout drafted a separate legal document binding his sons, Horatio and Samuel, to comply with the terms of his will and its codicils.[54] Ridout also asked his wife to honor his wishes: Mary Ridout wrote to her mother that "he said Ruth and Charity had been two such faithful servants that he desired more might be done for them than the rest. That if I survived him he requested me if they were living to leave them a small annuity to maintain them comfortably."[55] In 1808, when Mary Ridout died, she bequeathed to Folks her "wearing apparel and feather bed" as well as one hundred dollars.[56]

Manumitted women entered a society that was quickly developing a class divide. Free women who lacked pensions or other beneficial relationships with patrons supported themselves in a variety of ways, including renting out rooms to boarders, taking in laundry, and selling goods. Despite the fact that she owned property, Charity Folks continued to work for the Ridout family. Both Charity Bishop and her niece, Elizabeth Folks, earned wages by working as domestics or doing piecework.[57] According to Rockman, a small minority of free black women also worked as prostitutes, thereby continuing their sexual exploitation to survive.[58]

Manumitted blacks encountered economic barriers and white racism that limited wealth to just a few dozen families.[59] Free blacks frequently pursued the same occupations they had performed in slavery, but working for wages meant competing with whites for employment. Free blacks often encountered aggression from whites who objected to black competitors or who found them too "uppity."[60] Many manumitted slaves, like Charity Folks, returned to their former owners as wage laborers. After Hercules Brice was freed, he continued to work at Hampton Plantation, cradling grain and doing other related jobs.[61]

During the early nineteenth century, African Americans were denied the right to put their savings in homesteads and building associations.[62] According to Jeffrey Brackett, lawmakers in Maryland attempted to pass legislation denying slaves emancipated after 1831 the right to purchase real estate.[63] As Dorsey points out, the Maryland government legislated dependency by denying African Americans the means to pursue economic self-sufficiency.[64]

Black men achieved the most prosperity in occupations that required specialized training, such as blacksmith, bricklayer, or builder.[65] Other free blacks did well by opening shops and offering their services as shoemakers, barbers, or bakers.[66] Others built their fortune in service professions. William Bishop, for example, inherited a carting business from his father and built it into a well-respected establishment.[67] Dr. John Ridout, the grandson of John Ridout, hired Bishop to carry goods from his home and office.[68] Success for men such as Bishop also meant depending on the patronage and social acceptance of prominent white southerners.[69] Bishop expanded his economic base by renting out property he either bought or inherited from his white father or from his mother-in-law and by the end of his life had become quite wealthy. William Calderhead estimates that William Bishop was the wealthiest free black in Anne Arundel County and one of the twelve richest men in Annapolis.[70]

The most complicated form of property ownership for free blacks was the practice of owning other people. In the Upper South, African Americans tended to own people to protect them from being sold away: Edward Boothe, for example, owned and later freed his grandson.[71] In the Lower South, however, free blacks were more likely to own slaves with the intention of profiting from their labor. Class divides were exacerbated when former enslaved individuals become slaveholders.[72] In 1830, some 653 free blacks in the Chesapeake owned 1,175 slaves, while in the Lower South, 2,128 free black individuals owned 4,728 bondpeople.[73]

Thomas and Charity Folks owned slaves to whom the Folkses' relationship is not clear. In 1804, Thomas Folks freed Sam Heywood in exchange for one hundred dollars, while his widow appears in the 1820 Census as the owner of one slave.[74] It is possible that the Census enumerator made a mistake, labeling one of her free kin as an enslaved person, or that the slave listed was one of the Calder children who had not yet finished the term of slavery stipulated by Mary Ridout. However, ten years later, three bondpeople resided in the Folks household, well after her grandchildren would have been manumitted.[75] Folks's granddaughter, Elizabeth, owned one person.[76] The Folkses' neighbors also owned small numbers of slaves, and slaves owned by blacks ran the same risk of being sold as did slaves owned by whites if cash was needed.[77] Thus, another complexity faced by free black households was the fact that the precarious nature of their freedom in a slave society required them to enslave others. And slaveholding offered no guarantees against financial reversals. In 1804, Thomas Folks was listed as an insolvent debtor and ordered to serve time in prison.[78]

Prosperous free blacks understood the importance of protecting wealth for future generations. When Charity Folks died, she left real estate to each of her three surviving daughters and one granddaughter.[79] A stroke had left her paralyzed in early 1834, when she was nearly seventy-five.[80] She regained her ability to walk and some ability to speak but died within a year. Although writing a will was not universal, even among white men, Folks did so, underscoring the importance that she attached to both property and kin.[81]

Folks also kept careful track of the debts she was owed. She bequeathed to her granddaughter, Elizabeth, "one hundred and eighty dollars due to me from Mr. Samuel Ridout and all the interest thereon at the time of my death."[82] This sort of financial acumen may account, at least in part, for why Folks's success as a property owner overshadows her life in bondage. She had a clear understanding of how to succeed in free society and worked hard to do so. Though she lacked formal education, Folks learned legal and business practices by observing the actions of those around her.

The combined wealth of the Folkses and Bishops made Charity's descendants one of the wealthiest black families in Annapolis.[83] Charity Bishop consolidated property she inherited from her mother and her husband and also acquired additional property, owning fourteen rental properties by 1880.[84] Other family members followed her lead. Somewhat oddly, however, in 1870, William and Charity Bishop sold some of Thomas and Charity Folks's property back to the Ridout family.[85] Orlando Ridout IV surmised that the Bishops sold the property in exchange for Dr. John Ridout's willingness to share aspects of his medical training with either their son, Nicholas Bishop, or their grandson, William Bishop.[86]

Charity Folks's descendants became part of the group of free African Americans known as the beige aristocracy. In Ira Berlin's view, "A degree of color consciousness had probably always existed among Southern free negroes."[87] It is unclear how this phenomenon played out in the lives of the Bishops and others, but it is a mistake to assume it did not exist. Class standing meant much to African Americans as they tried to distance themselves from their enslaved experience.

For some manumitted women, freedom meant economic success; many more, however, experienced slavery's long reach even in their new lives. As Nell Irvin Painter points out, there is no way to come to a "fully loaded cost accounting of slavery."[88]

Apprenticeships and the Gendering of Poverty

Being part of the rising free black class did little to protect the Bishops and other members of the beige aristocracy against legal barriers and racism. Freeborn and recently liberated African Americans existed in a state of uneasiness.[89] They lived under curfews and were forced to register and carry freedom certificates listing their county of birth, thereby marking those who traveled in search of employment as outsiders.[90] Maryland's free blacks found their legal standing declining as their numbers increased, so that by midcentury, even Baltimore City had begun to lose its reputation as a safe haven.[91]

In 1818, the state of Maryland authorized the judges of the orphans' courts to bind out the children of "free negroes and mulattoes."[92] By 1825, "the children of any free negroes or mulattoes, not having visible means of supporting them, may be bound out by the orphans court as apprentices."[93] On the Eastern Shore, manumitted parents could wait seven years or more to see their apprenticed children enjoy their freedom.[94]

From 1820 to 1850, the Anne Arundel County Court bound 46 black children and 421 white children into apprenticeships.[95] Both white and black parents sought to provide their children with training that would ensure their economic mobility. However, white youth became more likely to learn basic skills as part of their apprenticeship. In Baltimore before 1820, 43 percent of African American boys who were apprenticed learned arithmetic, while 83 percent of white children were taught to read.[96] However, according to T. Stephen Whitman, after 1820, when more African Americans began entering apprentice arrangements, educational components such as reading and "ciphering" stopped appearing in their agreements, while rudimentary education remained common for white apprentices. Jennifer Hull Dorsey has found similar results for the Eastern Shore.[97] Thus, education was already underdeveloped for free African Americans, and this trend continued into the next century.

Free black parents took a proactive approach to apprenticeship arrangements to prevent the orphans' court from binding their children into unfavorable agreements, requesting that children be placed with particular black craftsmen.[98] Some parents traveled from as far as Talbot County to enter their children into apprenticeship arrangements with particular Baltimore master tradesmen.[99] Kinsey Johns petitioned on behalf of his nephew, Clem, "whose father is a slave and whose mother now deceased was a free woman."[100] With Clem's mother dead, he had no visible support, so his uncle sought to apprentice the boy to James Johns, Kinsey's brother and another of Clem's uncles.[101] George Barrow's mother consented for her son to be bound to John Wright, a white seaman who owned Barrow's husband.[102] By apprenticing their children to kinfolk or to familiar whites, parents and guardians sought to obtain some control over the conditions under which their children labored. In addition, the practice allowed artisans to pass their craft on to family members.

Some parents placed multiple children with the same master. Nanny Yealdhall consented to have three of her sons apprentice under Charles Mahoney, a wheelwright, who would provide food and housing until they turned twenty-one.[103] Between 1785 and 1790, "Negro Catherine" bound at least four of her children as apprentices to Absalom Butler: John and Thomas learned farming until they reached the age of twenty-one, while Violet learned the art of sewing and reading instruction "appropriate to her station in life" and would serve until she was sixteen. Butler also agreed to provide for any children born to Violet during her term.[104] Agreements generally included arrangements for babies born to apprenticed girls, though this one was unusual in that the master agreed to bear financial responsibility for those infants.

Men were more likely to receive freedom dues at the end of their apprenticeships, though in some cases women also received such payments. In November 1823, the Anne Arundel Orphans' Court bound ten-year-old Catherine Jones, a "colored orphan," until she reached age sixteen. In exchange for "conduct[ing] herself as a good and faithful apprentice," Jones would receive "good and sufficient meat, drinking, washing and lodging." At the conclusion of her term she would be paid freedom dues.[105] In August 1826, eleven-year-old Maria Toogood was bound to Albert Bentan to learn "the art and mystery of a seamstress" until she reached sixteen. At the end of her training she was to receive "freedom dues agreeable to an Act of Assembly."[106]

Apprenticeships guarded against poverty when parents' incomes were already spread thin. In 1826, Sarah, a free woman "without visible support," agreed to allow her eight-year-old son, Bope, to serve Benjamin Faulkner.[107] In 1814, Baltimorean Julia Norris gave permission for her son, Edward, to learn boot making from Solomon Johnson, who, like her, was a free African American. The agreement also called for Edward to receive "schooling, appropriate to his station in life."[108]

Apprenticeships not only ensured that children were cared for but also offered a means of economic mobility of some families. When Anne Arundel resident Rachel Dorsey died in 1819, Thomas Francis purchased his son, sixteen-year-old Samuel, from the estate and apprenticed him to William Hink, a blacksmith, for eight years.[109] Charity Folks's son-in-law, William Bishop II, had four siblings who were manumitted prior to the age of twenty-one and placed with local artisans. After serving a seven-year apprenticeship with a barber, Horace Bishop would receive a suit of clothing and thirty dollars. Although Horace Bishop was biracial, the court clerk listed him as white.[110]

A second generation of Bishops took advantage of apprenticeships as well. Moses Bishop, the son of William and Charity, signed on as a confectioner's trainee in 1850 and later went on to work as a cook at the U.S. Naval Academy.[111] Another son, William Bishop Jr., took on apprentices and trained them as barbers. The apprenticeship system helped make the Bishops some of the best-trained and wealthy blacks in Annapolis and Baltimore.

But apprenticeships also reinforced the state's power over domestic spaces. By 1834, master artisans were no longer required to educate apprentices in rudimentary writing and math. At the same time, African American children became disproportionately bound into the lowest forms of trade labor.[112] From the standpoint of Maryland lawmakers, the goal of apprenticing African American children was not to educate them but to check the black population's progress.

Orphans' courts, which were part of the county court system, often regulated apprenticeship disputes and contracts. These courts had initially managed the increase in orphaned, illegitimate, and landless white children in seventeenth-century Maryland.[113] By the early nineteenth century, they resolved estate disputes, settled guardian accounts, executed plans to alleviate the condition of the poor, and presided over apprenticeship arrangements. The number of free blacks appearing in the orphans' courts began to rise at the same time that white fears regarding an explosion in the number of free blacks were mushrooming.

To the extent that the poor relief system was overburdened, African Americans were not swelling the almshouse rolls. In the mid-1800s, whites outnumbered blacks in the Baltimore City almshouse by a ratio of nearly three to one.[114] These numbers suggest that local governments opposed rendering aid to the newly freed and largely impoverished black population unless that aid took the form of apprenticeships.

How did poverty become synonymous with free black women? Large numbers of African Americans did not people the almshouse. Men were traditionally more likely than women to enter apprenticeships, and this pattern held for Baltimore and Anne Arundel Counties from 1790 to 1830. Karen Zipf argues that the increased role of black women in the apprenticeship process during Reconstruction suggests that they exercised their rights as heads of their households.[115] However, beginning in the early national period, black women's interactions with the state in orphans' courts contributed to a gendered perception of poverty that has persisted for two hundred years. The same women who in bondage had produced children for the slave economy in freedom produced children depicted as in need of aid even though they were not eligible for that aid. In fact, needing aid would have sent them back to slavery because their mothers would have failed in their duty to feed, clothe, and support their children.

The combination of the legal apprenticeship structure with an upsurge in the number of freed slaves produced a series of dichotomies related to subjects and citizens. The nature of the social contract meant that U.S. citizens had a right to state assistance in exchange for their valuable contributions to society or to ensure their full participation in the polity.[116] However, in eighteenth- and nineteenth-century Maryland, black women were neither subjects nor citizens. Nevertheless, apprenticeships demonstrate that freed black women in the early republic were entrusted with the responsibility of raising productive "citizens." As Dorothy Roberts notes, "Liberty guards against government intrusion. It does not guarantee social justice."[117] Black women fell outside the traditional categories of "freedom" and "liberty" at the same time that their actions and those of their descendants structured dialogues about American slavery and American freedom in the developing nation. Maryland and other slave states crafted new laws that prevented future generations of enslaved people from acquiring freedom. In response, African American women exploited whatever loopholes were available to protect the future of their children.

Although the home was a site of freedom for African American women, slavery's tentacles still intruded. Some women harbored rage and resentment from their years in slavery. Others mourned children who were still enslaved. Still others, however, possessed moments of joy at having survived, although that joy was tempered by laws that aimed to circumscribe and control the free black population through real estate restrictions, curfews, vagrancy requirements. The household and the women in it bore witness to many of the truths of black life and anchored a community experiencing its first tastes of freedom.

CONCLUSION

Memorials and Reparations by the Living

> Follow after charity, and desire spiritual gifts,
> but rather that ye may prophesy.
> –I Corinthians 14:1 (KJV)

Charity Folks anticipated being lost to history. In her final years, she often felt displaced and feared being "turned out of doors." She obsessively searched for something lost, and "half of the time she did not know what she was after." Family members and neighbors described her as "deranged."[1] Given her age, her poor health, and the trauma of her past, it is probably not surprising that Folks suffered from symptoms associated with dementia.

The ailing Folks moved in with her daughter, Charity, and her husband, William Bishop, leading to a feeling of rootlessness that was exacerbated by her sense that Bishop was eclipsing her as the family's leader.[2] During one fight between Bishop and Folks, she remarked that "that there was no other place for her" and "set off to the graveyard."[3] The records of an 1835 legal dispute provide the last public documentation of Charity Folks's life.

For a long time, Charity Folks's final resting place remained a mystery. One theory held that she was interred with John and Mary Ridout at Whitehall. The Ridouts were buried without headstones, as John Ridout believed that their graves might be vulnerable to robbers. Portions of Whitehall have since been sold, and the exact location of the graves has been lost. But a family genealogical chart bears the notation that Charity Folks, "the wife of Thomas, personal maid to the wife of the governor," is buried in St. Anne's Cemetery.[4] Tucked away between the Severn River and Route 150, St. Anne's connects historic Annapolis with the modern world, containing graves spanning two hundred years of the city's history.[5] In the Bishop family plot, the lettering on Thomas Folks's gravestone is no longer visible but must be traced with one's fingertips. Next to

Thomas is a grave that lacks a headstone and has a footstone with lettering even more worn than that on Thomas's marker—so worn that I was unable to decipher it, even by photographing it and making rubbings of it. But in the spring of 2013, as the bright sun struck the grave from just the right angle, some of the lettering became just barely visible: *C. Folks, 183*, followed by either a 1 or a 4.

Charity Folks's life continues to claim our attention. The Belair Plantation where she may have been born is now part of the City of Bowie Museums. Tours of Belair have recently incorporated references to the bondpeople who worked there. The John Ridout house at 120 Duke of Gloucester Street in Annapolis is privately owned by a member of the Ridout family. Reynolds Tavern, once owned by the Davidson family that enslaved Thomas Folks, is now a tourist site popular for its afternoon tea and dinner. Some of the outlines of Charity Folks's presence are fainter. Her home on the corner of Duke of Gloucester Street and Church Circle no longer exists; it has been replaced by a Bank of America building. Other properties that she or William Bishop owned are now sites of archeological digs, continuing to yield crucial details about Annapolis. During the late nineteenth century, Folks's property at 84 Franklin Street was sold to the Mount Moriah African Methodist Episcopal Church, which constructed a new sanctuary on the site. Frederick Douglass delivered the dedication address when the church opened its doors in 1874. Added to the National Register of Historic Places in 1973, Mount Moriah has been converted into the Banneker-Douglass Museum, Maryland's official repository for African American heritage.[6]

Maryland's ghosts of slavery are now starting to be heard. In 2004, for example, members of the Haley and Ridout families participated in a "Reconciliation March" in response to a series of race-based incidents in Anne Arundel County.[7] Participants began at the Annapolis docks, where Kunta Kinte first touched American soil, and ended at the Maryland State House, where descendants of Alex Haley and John Ridout embraced and made public statements in support of the idea that race relations can be healed if both sides are willing to recognize the truth of the past.

The Haley family continues in the tradition of Kunta Kinte by stressing the importance of knowing one's past. Alex Haley's nephew, Christopher Haley, is the director of the Study for the Legacy of Slavery in Maryland Project. He and other members of his family continue to honor the legacies of Kunta Kinte and Alex Haley by serving on the board of the Kunta Kinte–Alex Haley Foundation, which promotes research designed to instill in all people a desire to rediscover their own "roots" and cultural heritage.[8] In 1981, the foundation erected a memorial to Alex Haley in the Annapolis Harbor, but the plaque was stolen less than forty-eight hours later and replaced by a card indicating that the Ku Klux Klan had visited the site.[9] The memorial has not been recovered.

The Ridouts, too, are working to heal the wounds of the past by preserving Maryland's history. Orlando Ridout IV continues his work on the advisory committee of the Kunta Kinte–Alex Haley Foundation and other noted historical organizations.[10] The late Orlando Ridout V authored works dedicated to reconstructing the architecture of Marylanders from diverse backgrounds. His sister, Mollie Ridout, works for the Historic Annapolis Foundation.

The state of Maryland is addressing its long legacy of slavery and racial discrimination. On March 26, 2007, legislators issued a formal apology in which they expressed "profound regret" that the state had once "trafficked in human flesh."[11] Two months later, the city of Annapolis adopted a similar resolution, noting that the "legacy of slavery continues to burden the life of our country and our community."[12]

Steps toward atonement are present in pedagogy as well. During the 2008–9 academic year, undergraduates in Ira Berlin's course at the University of Maryland, College Park, researched the institution's ties to slavery, published a blog as well as a forty-nine-page document detailing their findings, and made recommendations to university president C. D. Mote Jr. Students discovered that at least sixteen of the university's original twenty-four trustees owned slaves. While they found no "concrete" relationship between the institution and slavery, according to Berlin, "If slaves didn't lay the bricks, they made the bricks. If they didn't make the bricks, they drove the wagon that brought the bricks. If they didn't drive the wagon, they built the wagon wheels." Students recommended that the university add more courses on slavery to the curriculum and that it honor the African Americans whose labor built the institution by listing them as "founders." The university took these recommendations under advisement but has issued no official apology.[13]

Symbolic gestures such as marches and formal apologies cannot wipe away the pain of slavery. They can, however, cast it in a new light by opening dialogues about social inequalities worldwide. In August 2004, the National Underground Railroad Freedom Center opened its doors in Cincinnati, focusing on "America's battle to rid itself of the ugly scourge of slavery and treat all its citizens with respect and dignity."[14] Efforts to build a National Slavery Museum in Virginia have stalled as a consequence of funding problems.[15]

In her descendants, Charity Folks has left a legacy greater than her material wealth or the places commemorated as historically significant. Folks's son-in-law, William Bishop (1802–70), was one of the twelve wealthiest men in Annapolis.[16] William's wife, Charity Bishop, owned sixteen properties at the time of her death.[17] The Bishops' only daughter, Rebecca (1830–54) married Peter Vogelsang of New York, and they became pillars of New York society. Their daughter, Theresa Vogelsang (1854–88), married Josiah T. Settle (1850–1915), a prominent lawyer and businessman from Mississippi. The Settles lived in Tennessee, where they owned a boardinghouse whose residents included antilynching activist and newspaper editor Ida B. Wells.[18]

William and Charity Bishop's sons also became prominent in their fields. James Calder Bishop (1824–93) ran a tobacco shop and added to his father's considerable property holdings.[19] Moses Lake Bishop (1833–69) served as a cook and cabin steward on the USS *Constitution*.[20] William Henry Bishop III (1824–1906) and his wife, Elizabeth Chew Bishop (d. 1886), helped establish St. Mary's Parish Church in Baltimore, one of the city's most significant African American congregations.[21] Their son, Dr. Hutchens Chew Bishop (1858–1937), served as the rector of St. Philip's Episcopal Church in New York City's Harlem, one of the country's largest and most important.[22]

Hutchens Chew Bishop inherited his great-grandmother's penchant for acquiring property through shrewd business tactics. Working with Harlem businessman John Nail, Bishop passed for white so that he could purchase real estate on 135th Street in Harlem.[23] Bishop and Nail then rented or deeded the property to African Americans, enabling them to circumvent the city's measures designed to prevent blacks from moving uptown.[24] Bishop also secured enough property to move St. Philip's Church from its original location on Mulberry Street in the Tenderloin District to 136th Street.[25] In 1917, St. Philip's was the coordinating center for "Silent Protest Parade," a march organized in response to the murder of African Americans in East St. Louis, Illinois.[26] Among the march organizers were W. E. B. Du Bois, James Weldon Johnson, and Countee Cullen.

Shelton Hale Bishop (1889–1957) succeeded his father as rector of St. Philip's, furthering his efforts to strengthen the Harlem community. Shelton Hale Bishop oversaw the church's efforts to develop the Lafargue Clinic, dedicated to African American mental health.[27]

Some of Charity Folks's descendants have emulated her work as a healer. Dr. Elizabeth Bishop Davis Trussell (1920–2010), the daughter of Shelton Hale Bishop and Eloise Carey, had a long and distinguished career as a professor of clinical psychiatry at Columbia University. She founded the Department of Psychiatry at Harlem Hospital Center, one of the country's first community-centered mental health facilities.[28]

Twelve members of Charity Folks's family rest in the plot. Their headstones mark a history that spans four centuries. Some graves are well maintained, while others threaten to fade into the past. Charity Bishop's headstone, for example, will snap at its base if it is not soon restored. Here, on a December afternoon when a blizzard threatened, I placed two sets of flowers—one at the base of the headstone for Charity Folks Bishop, the other in the empty space between the headstones for Thomas Folks and his daughter, Mary. Two centuries after her death, Charity Folks was remembered.

EPILOGUE

When I submitted this manuscript to the press, I felt unsettled. The book was finished but not complete. I felt compelled (in truth, guided) to find and meet Liberty Rashad, the granddaughter of the Reverend Shelton Hale Bishop and the daughter of Dr. Elizabeth Bishop Davis Trussell. I learned of Liberty's existence from Gail Silver of St. Philip's Episcopal Church and contacted Liberty with the assistance of Vanderbilt University historian Dennis Dickerson and Dorothy Patton, a cousin of Liberty's.

The first time we spoke, in December 2012, I told her that *Liberty* is an appropriate name for the descendant of freedom fighters. The irony was not lost on either of us. As we spoke about her ancestor, Charity Folks, we quickly realized that we were talking about two different women. Liberty was well versed in the history of Charity Folks Bishop but had never heard of Charity Folks. She was even lost to her family.

On Easter Sunday 2013, I met Liberty and her family on the Annapolis dock by the Alex Haley memorial. She had never before visited the city. We spent the day touring and trading stories about her ancestors. As we walked past the Ridout house, a man came out and Liberty struck up a conversation. Clayton Struse explained that his wife was a member of the Ridout family, and when he learned that Liberty was a descendant of Charity Folks, he invited us in and showed us around the house and garden. He told us about the family history written by Joan Scurlock and plays about Charity Folks written by Janice Hayes-Williams. In fact, he said, children at the local elementary school often dress up like Charity Folks for history programs.

Liberty and I spent two additional days retracing her family's past. The trip was profound, blessed by the ancestors, and it exceeded our expectations. Charity's presence was everywhere. We felt her when we entered the John Ridout house, at the Banneker-Douglass Museum, as we stood in front of the Bank of America building. We felt her as we entered St. Mary's Catholic Church. We snapped photos and toasted her memory.

We ended our visit at the Bishop family plot at St. Anne's Cemetery. Liberty placed flowers honoring her ancestors and called out their names. It was then that the lettering on the worn footstone was revealed. Charity wanted to be remembered by her family.

Charity Folks and other African American women living at the turn of the nineteenth century used three tactics to move the boundaries of freedom in slavery and to withstand the movement of slavery into freedom. These mechanisms are unquantifiable, yet they nourished black women and gave them the strength to withstand gender, racial, and class barriers. The first is faith. Enslaved women had faith that they might experience moments of happiness as free persons. The second is hope. They hoped that legal documents would follow the verbal promise of freedom. The third is love. In his first epistle to the Corinthians, Paul emphasized that love includes being patient, being kind, speaking truthfully, and using one's spiritual gifts to help and heal others. In modern translations of the Bible, the word *charity* is replaced by the word love. As this book suggests, any interpretation of slavery that omits love (or in this case, Charity) may misrepresent the motivations of enslaved women who pursued freedom for themselves, for their kin, and ultimately for their descendants. Black women leaned on faith, hope, and love singularly and collectively. Even in dark times, when hope was lost and faith was questioned, love remained.

If the story of Charity Folks and other enslaved women is any indication, what we do matters. The stories of enslaved women and black women more generally are crucial to our understanding of the long arc of the fight for freedom. I like to believe that Charity Folks is finding peace. She rests at the center of the family plot, surviving the ebb and flow of time, encircled by all her folk. The tombstones of her husband, Thomas; her daughters, Mary Norris Lake and Charity Bishop; and her son-in-law, William Bishop, bear witness to the family's enslaved past. As she hoped, her grandchildren, Moses Lake Bishop and Charity Bishop Vogelsang, and her great-grandchildren, John T. Bishop and Dr. William Bishop, experienced lives of freedom. She and her descendants testify to the unconquerable spirit of survival and adaptation among enslaved people. Charity Folks seems to call out from the past, triumphantly proclaiming, "Despite it all, we are still here."

NOTES

Abbreviations

AACCMR	Anne Arundel County Court, Manumission Records, Archives of Maryland Online, Maryland State Archives
AACCRW	Anne Arundel County Court, Register of Wills (Indentures), Archives of Maryland, Maryland State Archives
HNHS	Hampton National Historic Site
Lake v. Bishop	*Moses Lake and Mary Lake v. William Bishop and Charity Bishop*, August 6, 1835, Anne Arundel County Court, Chancery Papers, Maryland State Archives
MdSA	Maryland State Archives
PHV	Race, Slavery, and Free Blacks, Series II: Petitions to Southern County Courts, Part B: Maryland (1775–1866), Delaware (1779–1857), District of Columbia (1803–1865), Slavery and the Law, Proquest History Vault, 2012

Prologue. The Ghosts of Slavery

1. Michel-Rolph Trouillot writes, "Slavery is a ghost, both the past and living presence; and the problem of historical representation is how to represent that ghost, something that is and yet is not" (quoted in Bailey, *African Voices*, 25). On ghosts of slavery and the lived experiences of the enslaved women referenced, see Sharpe, *Ghosts of Slavery*; Altink, *Representations of Slave Women*; Braxton and Diedrich, *Monuments of the Black Atlantic*; Brooks, *Bodies in Dissent*; Crais and Scully, *Sara Baartman*; Gordon-Reed, *Hemingses of Monticello*; Hartman, *Scenes of Subjection*; Miles, *House on Diamond Hill*; Morrison, *Beloved*; Morrison, *Playing in the Dark*; John, *Unburnable*; McLaurin, *Celia, a Slave*; Mair and Ranston, *Rebel Woman*; Reinhardt, *Who Speaks for Margaret Garner?*; Painter, *Sojourner Truth*; Washington, *Sojourner Truth's America*.

2. Charity Folks, Certificate of Freedom, April 29, 1811, Anne Arundel County Court, Certificates of Freedom, 823:8, MdSA.

3. Joan C. Scurlock, "The Bishop Family of Annapolis," unpublished manuscript, 1999, 5, Banneker-Douglass Museum.

4. Millward, "Charity Folks," 24.

5. Charity Folks, Last Will and Testament, 1828, AACCRW. See also Millward, "Charity Folks," 35–36.

6. For works on black families and uplift, see Grimké, *Journals of Charlotte Forten*

Grimké; Rudd and Bond, *From Slavery to Wealth*; Adele Logan Alexander, *Homelands and Waterways*; Adele Logan Alexander, *Parallel Worlds*; Hayre and Moore, *Tell Them We Are Rising*. For other readings of African American families who considered themselves elite, see Gatewood, *Aristocrats of Color*; Winch, *Clamorgans*.

7. Millward, "Charity Folks," 24.

8. Mary Ridout, Manumission Record for Charity Folks, December 6, 1797, AACCMR, 825:17–18; Mary Ridout, Manumission Record for Charity Folks and Others, August 1807, AACCMR, 830:2–6; Calderhead, "Slavery in Maryland."

9. For descriptions of the John Ridout house and garden, see Leone, *Archaeology of Liberty*; Shackel and Little, *Historical Archaeology of the Chesapeake*.

10. Scurlock, "Bishop Family of Annapolis"; Janice Hayes-Williams, conversation with author, November 1, 2009, Annapolis, Md.

11. Millward, "Charity Folks," 26.

12. "Statue Dedication Ceremony for Frederick Douglass," on Website of Speaker of the House John Boehner, http://www.speaker.gov/frederickdouglass/.

13. Frederick Douglass–Isaac Myers Maritime Park, Baltimore, http://www.douglassmyers.org/visitorinfo.php.

14. Millward, "Charity Folks," 27.

15. Whitman, "Manumission and Apprenticeship," 56 n. 5.

16. Hershini Bhana Young, *Haunting Capital*, 1. Young speaks in particular about the diaspora being embedded in memory.

Introduction. Moving Freedom, Shaping Slavery

1. Adams and Pleck, *Love of Freedom*; Dunbar, *Fragile Freedom*; Hanger, *Bounded Lives, Bounded Places*; King, *Essence of Liberty*; Myers, *Forging Freedom*; Schweninger, "Fragile Nature of Freedom"; Shirley Elizabeth Thompson, *Exiles at Home*.

2. Schweninger, "Fragile Nature of Freedom," 107.

3. Cowling, "Negotiating Freedom." See also King, "Out of Bounds"; Schweninger, "Fragile Nature of Freedom."

4. See Quarles, *Negro in the American Revolution*; David Brion Davis, *Problem of Slavery in the Age of Revolution*; Frey, *Water from the Rock*; Isaacs, *Transformation of Virginia*; Nash, *Urban Crucible*; Pybus, *Epic Journeys of Freedom*. See also Norton, "Fate of Some Black Loyalists"; Frey, "Between Slavery and Freedom."

5. Quarles, *Negro in the American Revolution*, especially 182–200.

6. Norton, "Fate of Some Black Loyalists." See also Norton, Gutman, and Berlin, "Afro-American Family."

7. Jacqueline Jones, "Mixed Legacy," 96–100.

8. Frey, *Water from the Rock*; Pybus, *Epic Journeys of Freedom*.

9. Dunbar, *Fragile Freedom*.

10. Adams and Pleck, *Love of Freedom*.

11. Cooper, *Hanging of Angélique*.

12. See Spruill, *Women's Life and Work*; Angela Davis, "Reflections"; Angela Davis, *Women, Race and Class*; Hine and Wittenstein, "Female Slave Resistance"; Bynum, *Unruly Women*; Clinton, *Plantation Mistress*; Fox-Genovese, *Within the Plantation Household*.

13. White, *Ar'n't I a Woman?*, 167.
14. Leslie Alexander, "Challenge of Race," 53. See also Shohat, *Talking Visions*.
15. Steady, *Black Women, Globalization*; Lee, *For Freedom's Sake*; Ula Taylor, *Veiled Garvey*; Ransby, *Ella Baker*.
16. Ula Taylor, "Feminism."
17. For similar discussions of African American women and post–Civil War society, see Edwards, *Gendered Strife and Confusion*; Saville, *Work of Reconstruction*; Glymph, *Out of the House*; Hunter, *To 'Joy My Freedom*.
18. Fields, *Slavery and Freedom*, 13. See also Rockman, *Scraping By*; Whitman, *Price of Freedom*; U.S. Census, 1790, 1830, 1860.
19. Jennifer Hull Dorsey, *Hirelings*; Grivno, *Gleanings of Freedom*; Schermerhorn, *Money over Mastery*.
20. Condon, "Slave Owner's Family"; Fields, *Slavery and Freedom*; Phillips, *Freedom's Port*; Rockman, *Scraping By*; Whitman, *Price of Freedom*.
21. Fields, *Slavery and Freedom*, 4–5.
22. I use Baltimore City/Baltimore Town and Baltimore County to distinguish the specific areas being discussed.
23. U.S. Census, 1790, 1830; Fields, *Slavery and Freedom*, 13.
24. Phillips, *Freedom's Port*, 4.
25. This designation of the Age of Revolution is based on the definition outlined by David Brion Davis. It covers the years and events leading to the American Revolution, the British abolition movement, and the final phases of the liberation of Saint-Domingue from French rule. See David Brion Davis, *Problem of Slavery in the Age of Revolution*; David Brion Davis, *Inhumane Bondage*.
26. Walter Johnson, "On Agency," 114.
27. Myers, *Forging Freedom*, 18, 11.
28. Fox-Genovese, *Within the Plantation Household*; Glymph, *Out of the House*.
29. Pargas, *Quarters and the Fields*, 8.
30. Myers, *Forging Freedom*, 18.
31. Jacqueline Jones, "Mixed Legacy," 96–100.
32. Philip D. Morgan suggests that nowhere is the expansion and contraction of freedom in the revolutionary period better captured than in the Chesapeake region (*Slave Counterpoint*, 512–14).
33. Berlin, *Many Thousands Gone*, 13–14. Likewise, Berlin suggests that the meaning of race changed, thus hastening a change in the meaning of slavery.
34. Kamoie, *Irons in the Fire*; Whitman, *Price of Freedom*; Rockman, *Scraping By*; Kaye, *Joining Spaces*; Camp, *Closer to Freedom*.
35. Wallace, "Fair Daughters of Africa," 18. Wallace is speaking specifically about the years between 1800 and 1860.
36. Berlin, *Slaves without Masters*, 51–78; Franklin and Schweninger, *Runaway Slaves*, 129; Barnes, *Baltimore Town*.
37. Anne Arundel County, Federal Direct Tax List, 1798, MdSA.
38. Ira Berlin and Philip D. Morgan, introduction to *Cultivation and Culture*, ed. Berlin and Morgan, 1.
39. Thomas Foote interview in Rawick, *American Slave*, 16:14; Fett, *Working Cures*.
40. "Occupations at Hampton," Kent Lancaster Papers, HNHS.

41. Berlin, *Many Thousands Gone*, 267.
42. Fett, *Working Cures*.
43. Rucker, *River Flows On*; Levine, *Black Culture and Black Consciousness*; Raboteau, *Slave Religion*.
44. The Ridout home was in close proximity to the establishment of William Faris, an Annapolis silversmith who wrote in his diary about trading herbs with free blacks and enslaved people. See Faris, *Diary of William Faris*, 380–90.
45. Kamoie, *Irons in the Fire*, 166–71.
46. "Ridgely Workers," "Jobs, ca. Death of Governor Ridgely," both in Lancaster Papers.
47. "Ridgely Workers," "Jobs, ca., Death of Governor Ridgely," both in Lancaster Papers. See also Bezís-Selfa, *Forging America*; Kamoie, *Irons in the Fire*, 166.
48. Bezís-Selfa, *Forging America*, 85.
49. "Jobs, ca., Death of Governor Ridgely," HNHS; Kamoie, *Irons in the Fire*, 166.
50. See especially Pargas, *Quarters and the Fields*; Grivno, *Gleanings of Freedom*.
51. Fields, *Slavery and Freedom*, 40.
52. Douglass, *Narrative*, 275.
53. For analysis of Douglass's observation on free black life in Baltimore, see Fields, *Slavery and Freedom*, 40–61; Phillips, *Freedom's Port*, 58–61.
54. Entry for March 28, 1838, in Blackford, *Ferry Hill Plantation Journal*, 20.
55. See especially Rockman, "Women's Labor."
56. Joseph Corbel Martiner, Manumission Record for "Negro Arsene" [Popettenon], January 1814, Baltimore County Court, Chattel Records, MdSA.
57. Dataset created by author.
58. John Davidson Daybook, June 5, 1782, MdSA. Tom also appears in John Davidson Account Book, Library of Congress. The account book reconciled household expenses as well as transactions occurring in the Davidson store. At the time she published her research on Davidson's account book, Lorena Walsh was unable to determine whether or not the Tom listed in Davidson's account book was an indentured servant, slave, or free black. The Tom who appears in Davidson's account book and daybook is the same as the Thomas Folks who was manumitted at Davidson's death in 1794 as well as the Tom Fowkes to whom John Ridout refers in the 1791 manumission deed for Mary Folks. See John Davidson, Manumission Record for Thomas Folks, 1794, Anne Arundel County Court, Land Records, MdSA; John Ridout, Manumission Record for Mary Folks, 1791, AACCMR; Walsh, *Provisioning Early American Towns*; Walsh, "Feeding the Eighteenth-Century Town Folk," 267; Walsh, "Urban Amenities and Rural Sufficiency," 109.
59. Orlando Ridout IV, conversation with author, December 16, 2009, Annapolis, Md.; Janice Hayes-Williams, conversation with author, November 1, 2009, Annapolis, Md. See also Joan C. Scurlock, "The Bishop Family of Annapolis," unpublished manuscript, 1999, 5, Banneker-Douglass Museum.
60. Camp, *Closer to Freedom*, 15.
61. James V. Deane interview in Rawick, *American Slave*, 16:8.
62. See Berry, "Swing the Sickle," 60–61.
63. Kilty, *Index to the Laws of Maryland*. For other examples in Virginia, see Hening, *Statutes at Large*, 308–9.

64. An Act to Prevent Disabled and Superannuated Slaves Being Set Free, or the Manumission of Slaves by Any Last Will or Testament, 1790, Archives of Maryland Online http://msa.maryland.gov/megafile/msa/speccol/sc2900/sc2908/000001/000204/html/am204—458.html.

65. See Daniels, "Alternative Workers"; Daniels, "WANTED"; Russo, "Chesapeake Artisans"; Carr, "Development."

66. Leone, *Archaeology of Liberty*, especially 182–244.

67. Levine, *Black Culture and Black Consciousness*; McDaniel and Johnson, *Africana Legacy*; Raboteau, *Slave Religion*.

68. Leone, *Archaeology of Liberty*, 182–244.

69. See, for example, Bascom, *Shango in the New World*; Lum, *Praising His Name*; Rucker, *River Flows On*.

70. Hartman, *Lose Your Mother*, 6.

71. Moynihan, *Negro Family*, especially chap. 4, "A Tangle of Pathology."

Chapter 1. Reproduction and Motherhood in Slavery, 1757–1830

1. Turner, "Home-Grown Slaves."

2. Cowling, "Debating Womanhood, Defining Freedom."

3. Camp, *Closer to Freedom*, 3.

4. On interracial sex and rape, see Pascoe, *What Comes Naturally*, 22; Warren, "More Than Words"; Block, *Rape and Sexual Power*; Hodes, *Sex, Love, Race*; Smith, *Sex without Consent*. For the development of the freed black class, see Adele Logan Alexander, *Homelands and Waterways*; Adele Logan Alexander, *Parallel Worlds*; Gatewood, *Aristocrats of Color*; Winch, *Clamorgans*.

5. Millward, "Relics of Slavery."

6. Boris, "From Gender to Racialized Gender," 9–13; Jennifer L. Morgan, "Some Could Suckle."

7. "1662 Law of Virginia," in Rose, *Documentary History of Slavery*, 16.

8. For similar laws in Maryland, see Millward, "Relics of Slavery," 24.

9. Kilty, *Index to the Laws of Maryland*, 1026.

10. Pascoe, *What Comes Naturally*, 22. Pascoe writes, "By using marriage to delineate race, lawmakers wrapped race in and around the gender differences that stood at the heart of nineteenth century marriage, which, in turn, stood at the heart of the American South."

11. Whitman, *Price of Freedom*.

12. Berlin, *Many Thousands Gone*, 13. See also Jennifer L. Morgan, *Laboring Women*; Brown, *Good Wives*.

13. Walter Johnson, *River of Dark Dreams*, 195.

14. Reddock, "Women and Slavery," 68.

15. Scholars of slavery have long seen this connection. For an overview of enslaved women's bodies and the reproduction of slavery, see Jennifer L. Morgan, *Laboring Women*; Roberts, *Killing the Black Body*; Weinbaum, "Gendering the General Strike."

16. Mustakeem, "She Must Go Overboard."

17. Turner, "Home-Grown Slaves."

18. Schwartz, *Birthing a Slave*, 144.
19. *Maryland Gazette*, February 2, 1772.
20. Cornelius Conaway to John Galloway, December 1780, Galloway-Maxcy-Markhoe Family Papers, Library of Congress.
21. Ibid., January 1781.
22. For a detailed discussion of Williams's experience, see White, *Ar'n't I a Woman?*, 102–3.
23. For a detailed discussion of breeding, see Berry, "Swing the Sickle," 77–84.
24. "Opinion of Daniel Dulany," in Catterall, *Judicial Cases*, 47.
25. Pennington, *Fugitive Blacksmith*, 5.
26. Block, *Rape and Sexual Power*, 68.
27. Boris, "From Gender to Racialized Gender"; Jennifer L. Morgan, "Some Could Suckle."
28. Millward, "More History Than Myth"; Roberts, *Killing the Black Body*.
29. Glymph, *Out of the House*, 4.
30. Richard Macks interview in Rawick, *American Slave*, 16:54–55.
31. Block, *Rape and Sexual Power*; Hodes, *White Women, Black Men*; Stevenson, "Distress and Discord"; Stevenson, "Gender Convention."
32. Brewer, "Entailing Aristocracy." Brewer argues that Virginia slavery was connected to an aristocratic ideology rather than a democratic one. Her analysis reveals that although entail declined in England, the practice rose in Tidewater Virginia. Thus, even smallholding male farmers found it increasingly difficult to hold property. White males were nonetheless protected by a variety of property laws that did not apply to women after they married.
33. Thomas Cockey to M. Cooke, November 1826, Thomas Cockey to C. Cockey, November 1826, both in Cockey Family Papers, MS 1782, Maryland Historical Society.
34. Thomas Cockey to M. Cooke, November 1826, Thomas Cockey to C. Cockey, November 1826, both in ibid.
35. See White's discussion of female slaves and self-sufficiency in *Ar'n't I a Woman?*, chap. 2. I appreciate Darlene Clark Hine's reminder of this crucial point.
36. See Cutrafelli, *Women of Africa*; Bush, *Slave Women*; Perrin, "Resisting Reproduction." For an in-depth discussion of slaves' birth control practices, see Du Bois, "Black Folks and Birth Control," 166–67. Cutrafelli suggests that slave women in Surinam induced abortions because the perverse breeding style of plantation owners mixed close family ties. Bush suggests that although sterility was a stigma in parts of West Africa, slave women nonetheless induced abortions in the New World to protest their enslaved status.
37. Blake, *Memoirs of Margaret Jane Blake*.
38. See White, *Ar'n't I a Woman?*, 15; Stevenson, "Gender Convention," 170–71; Reinhardt, *Who Speaks for Margaret Garner?*.
39. Stevenson, *Life in Black and White*, 245; White, *Ar'n't I a Woman?*, 125.
40. Reinhardt, "*Who Speaks for Margaret Garner?*," 104–5; Reinhardt, *Who Speaks for Margaret Garner?*
41. See Jennifer L. Morgan's chapter on Hannah and her daughters in *Laboring Women*, 107–44. See also Cutrafelli, *Women of Africa*, 180.

42. Bush, *Slave Women*, 120–49.
43. Cutrafelli, *Women of Africa*, 180.
44. White, *Ar'n't I a Woman?*, 119.
45. Douglass, *My Bondage and My Freedom*, 51.
46. See Blassingame, *Slave Community*; Genovese, *Roll, Jordan, Roll*; Gutman, *Black Family*; Kulikoff, Tobacco and Slaves; Stevenson, *Life in Black and White*; Hudson, *To Have and to Hold*.
47. Fox-Genovese, *Within the Plantation Household*; Stevenson, "Black Family Structure"; Jennifer L. Morgan, *Laboring Women*; Berry, "*Swing the Sickle*."
48. Stevenson, "Black Family Structure."
49. See Stevenson, *Life in Black and White*, especially section 2.
50. James V. Deane interview in Rawick, *American Slave*, 16:6–7.
51. Fields, *Slavery and Freedom*, 25.
52. John Hurt to John Galloway, November 25, 1781, Galloway-Maxcy-Markhoe Family Papers.
53. Thomas Randall Estate Inventory, Baltimore County Court, Chattel Records, MdSA.
54. Agreement between J. Galloway and R. Thomas, November 1790, Galloway-Maxcy-Markhoe Family Papers.
55. Ben Chambers to John Galloway, May 2, 1777, Galloway-Maxcy-Markhoe Family Papers.
56. Daniel Dulany Letter, 1768, Carroll Family Papers, Library of Congress.
57. Philip D. Morgan, *Slave Counterpoint*; Hudson, *To Have and to Hold*; Berlin, *Many Thousands Gone*.
58. Charles Carroll to J. Meredith, 1837, Carroll Family Papers.
59. Richard Sprigg Estate Inventory, 1798–99, Anne Arundel County Court, Estate Inventories, MdSA.
60. Walters, "Rediscovering the Cultural Milieu," 14. See also Frederickson, "Mother's Arithmetic."
61. Baltz, *Belair from the Beginning*, 34; Joan C. Scurlock, "The Bishop Family of Annapolis," unpublished manuscript, 1999, 5–8, Banneker-Douglass Museum.
62. Anne Tasker's parents were among the most prominent members of Chesapeake slaveholding society. Benjamin Tasker Sr. was a founder of the Baltimore County Ironworks, a mayor of Annapolis, and the provincial governor of Maryland from 1752 to 1753, and he profited from his active participation in the international slave trade. Anne Tasker's mother, Anne Bladen Tasker, also came from a family that included wealthy slaveholders, landowners, court officials, and governors. The extended branches of the family included not only the Ogles, Taskers, and Bladens but also the Carrolls, Carters, Dulanys, Ridgelys, and Snowdens, among others. Like most slave-owning families, the Taskers transferred their bondpeople between properties and family members as labor was needed.
63. Samuel Ogle Will, 1752, Wills and Death Duties, Public Records Office; Anne Ogle to Col. Benjamin Tasker, 1758 Deed to Belair, Robert Carter Papers, Virginia Historical Society; Samuel Ogle Estate Inventory, 1752, Carter Papers; Benjamin Ogle Estate Inventory, 1815, courtesy Pamela Williams Belair Mansion; Col. Benjamin Tasker

Jr. Estate Inventory, 1763, Carter Papers; *Benjamin Ogle v. Anne Ogle, Robert Carter, et al.*, 1774–75, Anne Arundel County Court, Chancery Papers, MdSA; Jean Russo, email to author, November 22, 2013.

64. "Rachel's Room," Pamela Williams Belair Mansion, July 14, 2010.

65. King, *Essence of Liberty*, 45. See also Dunbar, *Fragile Freedom*; Hanger, *Bounded Lives, Bounded Places*.

66. Ellison, "Resistance to Oppression," 56; King, *Stolen Childhood*.

67. Sterling, *We Are Your Sisters*, 56.

68. Warren, "Cause of Her Grief," 1031.

69. For the importance of the autobiographical story, see Stevenson, "Gender Ideals," 169–75.

70. Darlene Clark Hine, "Rape and the Inner Lives of Black Women: Thoughts on the Culture of Dissemblance," in *Hine Sight*, 37–48.

71. White, *Ar'n't I a Woman?*, 5.

72. Ward, *Autobiography of a Fugitive Negro*, 15–18.

73. King, *Essence of Liberty*, 45; Baptist, "Cuffy."

74. Clark, *Strange History*.

75. Ibid. See also Spear, *Race, Sex, and Social Order*.

76. Douglass, *Narrative*, 2.

77. See, for example, "Lucy Jackson," "Black Cemetery," both in Kent Lancaster Papers, HNHS; James Howard, Account of the Ridgely Family, HNHS. See also Lancaster, "Chattel Slavery."

78. Calvert, *Rosalie Stier Calvert*, 378–84.

79. Ibid., 380.

80. Brown, *Good Wives*, 237. See also Block, *Rape and Sexual Power*.

81. Scurlock, "Bishop Family of Annapolis"; Karimu Rashad, conversation with author, April 1, 2013, Annapolis, Md.

82. Scurlock, "Bishop Family of Annapolis," 11, 59; Liberty Rashad, conversation with author, April 1, 2013, Annapolis, Md.

83. Gordon-Reed, *Hemingses of Monticello*, 17.

84. Anne Ogle, Manumission Record for James, October 1789, AACCMR.

85. *Lake v. Bishop*, petition to remove gate and fence blocking an alley in Annapolis.

86. John Ridout, Last Will and Testament, 1797, Ridout Family Papers, MdSA; Mary Ridout, Manumission Record for Charity Folks, December 6, 1797, AACCMR, 825:17–18; Mary Ridout, Manumission Record for Charity Folks and Others, August 1807, AACCMR, 830:2–6; Charity Folks, Certificate of Freedom, 1811, Anne Arundel County Court, Certificates of Freedom, 823:8, MdSA; Mary Folks, Certificate of Freedom, 1811, Anne Arundel County Court, Certificates of Freedom, 823:7–8; Harriet Calder, Certificate of Freedom, 1811, Anne Arundel County Court, Certificates of Freedom, 823:9.

87. See White, *Ar'n't I A Woman?*, especially chaps. 1, 2.

88. Samuel Ogle Estate Inventory, 1752, Carter Papers; Benjamin Ogle Estate Inventory, 1815, courtesy Pamela Williams Belair Mansion; Col. Benjamin Tasker Jr., Estate Inventory, 1763, Anne Ogle to Benjamin Tasker, 1758 Deed to Belair, both in Carter Papers; *Benjamin Ogle v. Anne Ogle, Robert Carter, et al.* There are no known inventories for the Ridout papers.

89. Scurlock, "Bishop Family of Annapolis," 17.
90. James Jackson, Testimony, *Lake v. Bishop*.
91. Henry Folks, Certificate of Freedom, 1825, Anne Arundel County Court, Certificates of Freedom, 823:47. See also Mary Ridout, Manumission Record for Charity Folks, December 6, 1797, AACCMR, 825:17–18.
92. Maryland Tax List, 1783, MdSA; U.S. Census, 1790.

Chapter 2. Beyond Charity

1. Schweninger, "Freedom Suits."
2. Letty Ogleton and Her Five Children, Petition for Freedom, September 10, 1810, Prince George's County Court, Black Papers, MdSA. See also Accession #008967-002-1034, PHV.
3. Anthony, Petition for Freedom, September 10, 1810, Amy Ogleton, Petition for Freedom, September 10, 1810, Eliza Ogleton and Her Three Children, Petition for Freedom, September 10, 1810, Letty Ogleton and Her Five Children, Petition for Freedom, September 10, 1810, Amy and Daniel Ogleton, Petition for Freedom, September 10, 1810, Milly Ogleton, Petition for Freedom, September 10, 1810, Harry, Joan, Mary, Suckey and Nelly, Petition for Freedom, September 10, 1810, Charles and Francis Ogleton, Petition for Freedom, September 10, 1810, all in Prince George's County Court, Black Papers.
4. Prince George's County Court, Docket and Minutes Book, September 1810–April 1811, MdSA.
5. Schweninger, "Freedom Suits."
6. Rezin Ogleton, Freedom Affidavit, September 19, 1810, Prince George's County, Freedom Affidavits, 763:1.
7. See, for example, Papenfuse, "From Redcompense to Revolution"; Hodes, *White Women, Black Men*.
8. Millward, "That All Her Increase Shall Be Free." See also Cheryl I. Harris, "Whiteness as Property."
9. Schweninger, "Freedom Suits," 40.
10. Adams and Pleck, *Love of Freedom*, 132.
11. Fuente, "Slave Law and Claims-Making in Cuba," 346.
12. Edwards, "Enslaved Women and the Law," 305–6.
13. Cowling, "Debating Womanhood, Defining Freedom."
14. Egerton, *Death or Liberty*, 93–95.
15. Adams and Pleck, *Love of Freedom*, 127.
16. Schweninger, "Freedom Suits," 55.
17. Martha S. Jones, "Case of *Jean Baptiste*," 119.
18. Loren Schweninger, email to author, April 2, 2014.
19. Ibid.
20. Ibid.
21. Berlin, *Many Thousands Gone*, 280–82.
22. *Negro Lucy v. Williams*, May 1780 Session Minutes, June 1780 Session Minutes, *Sundry Negroes v. Hopewell & Others*, October 1780 Session Minutes, *Elizabeth Hopewell v. Negroes Nan, Frank, Mingle, Negro Isaac et al.*, May 1781 Session Minutes, *D. Samuel*

v. Freeborn Brown, May 1782 Session Minutes, *Ann Toogood*, October 1782 Session Minutes, May 1783 Session Minutes, *Dick Rofe and Priscilla Toogood*, May 1785 Session Minutes, *Negroes Nanny, Lydia, and Basil*, October 1785 Session Minutes, *Peter, Nancy, Lydia*, October 1786 Session Minutes, *Nanny and Lydia*, May 1787 Session Minutes, *Nancy Butler*, October 1787 Session Minutes, *Worthington v. Rachel*, October 1787 Session Minutes, *Nancy and Lydia*, May 1788 Session Minutes, all in General Court of the Western Shore, Minutes of the Proceedings, MdSA.

23. *Sarah Greene v. Charles Greene*, December 1784, Virginia House of Delegates, Accession #11678403, Abraham Peyton Skipwith Petition, November 1785, Virginia House of Delegates, Accession #11678506, Petition of James, November 1786, Virginia General Assembly, Accession #11678601, all in PHV.

24. *Eleanor Toogood v. Upton Scott*, August Term, 1782, General Court of the Western Shore, Appeals and Judgments, MdSA. See also Accession #20978201, PHV.

25. Hodes, *White Women, Black Men*, 19–38. See also Whitman, *Challenging Slavery in the Chesapeake*, 62–65.

26. Hodes, *White Women, Black Men*, 19–38.

27. Whitman, *Challenging Slavery in the Chesapeake*, 64.

28. Hodes, *White Women, Black Men*, 20; Whitman, *Challenging Slavery in the Chesapeake*, 80–81.

29. Hodes, *White Women, Black Men*, 20.

30. Schweninger, "Freedom Suits," 40–47; Whitman, *Challenging Slavery in the Chesapeake*, 82.

31. Schweninger, "Freedom Suits," 39–40. See also Schweninger, *Southern Debate over Slavery*, 165.

32. See Schweninger, "Freedom Suits."

33. Rabin, "In a Country of Liberty?"

34. Papenfuse, "From Redcompense to Revolution."

35. *Mahoney v. Ashton*, 1791–1802, Proceedings of the General Court of the Western Shore, Accession #20979115, PHV; Papenfuse, "From Redcompense to Revolution"; "Reverend John Ashton," Archives of Maryland Biography Series, http://msa.maryland.gov/megafile/msa/speccol/sc5400/sc5496/041700/041715/html/041715bio.html.

36. "Reverend John Ashton."

37. Ferrer, *Freedom's Mirror*; Scott, *Degrees of Freedom*.

38. Papenfuse, "From Redcompense to Revolution," 62.

39. Sweet, *Recreating Africa*; Sidbury, *Becoming African in America*; Dubois, *Avengers of the New World*.

40. Litwack, *Been in the Storm So Long*, especially chap. 1, "The Faithful Slave," 1–63.

41. Martha S. Jones, "Case of *Jean Baptiste*," 106.

42. *Margaret Creek v. William Wilkins*, Petition for Freedom, November 1797, General Court of the Western Shore, Accession #20979704, PHV.

43. Cowling, "Negotiating Freedom," 378.

44. *Richard Booth v. David Weems*, General Court of the Western Shore, Accession #20978908, PHV.

45. Ibid.

46. Ibid.

47. 1809 Law of Maryland, in Kilty, *Index to the Laws of Maryland*, 171.
48. For the most recent literature on bondwomen and reproduction, see Berry, "Swing the Sickle," 77–84; Jennifer L. Morgan, *Laboring Women*. For discussion of slave law, see Joseph C. Dorsey, "Women without History." For classic studies, see White, *Ar'n't I a Woman?*; Bush, *Slave Women*.
49. Whitman, *Price of Freedom*, 23.
50. Ibid., 123.
51. Leslie M. Harris, *In the Shadow of Slavery*, 23–25. See also Jennifer L. Morgan, "Gender and Slavery," 146; Herndon, *Unwelcome Americans*.
52. Whitman, *Price of Freedom*, 27.
53. Ibid., 123.
54. See Catterall, *Judicial Cases*; Digital Library on American Slavery, http://library.uncg.edu/slavery/petitions/; Jennifer Hull Dorsey, "Documentary History."
55. Millward, "That All Her Increase Shall Be Free," 376 n. 43.
56. Ibid.
57. Lurena and Ellen, Petition for Freedom, 1818, Accession #20981604, PHV.
58. African American networks included abroad marriages and were nuclear, matrifocal, matrilocal, fictive, and extended in scope. See Stevenson, "Black Family Structure"; Penningroth, *Claims of Kinfolk*. For the relationship between African cultural survival and Christianity, see Rucker, *River Flows On*; Frey and Wood, *Come Shouting to Zion*.
59. Washington, *Sojourner Truth's America*.
60. Schweninger, *Southern Debate over Slavery*, 165.
61. Susannah Williams, Petition, February 1806, Schweninger Collection, MdSA. See also Accession #20980604, PHV.
62. Susannah Williams, Manumission Record, 1805, AACCMR, 825:259. See also "Robert Williams," Archives of Maryland Biography Series, http://msa.maryland.gov/megafile/msa/speccol/sc3500/sc3520/016400/016404/html/16404bio.html.
63. Negro Joe, Petition for Freedom, 1832, Accession #20983202, PHV.
64. Myers, *Forging Freedom*, 127, 174.
65. Chester Coleman to John and Betsey, 1828, Frederick County Court, Petitions, MdSA.
66. Burin, *Peculiar Solution*; Clegg, *Price of Liberty*; Blackett, *Beating against the Barriers*; Mitchell, *Righteous Propagation*; Penelope Campbell, *Maryland in Africa*.
67. Sally Henry Petition, 1814, Accession #20481403, PHV.

Chapter 3. Commodities and Kin

1. Patterson, *Slavery and Social Death*.
2. See Dunbar, *Fragile Freedom*; Myers, *Forging Freedom*; Whitman, *Price of Freedom*; Rockman, *Scraping By*.
3. Nathans, *To Free a Family*; Heather Andrea Williams, *Help Me to Find My People*.
4. O'Malley, "Final Passages," 93–94.
5. Penningroth, *Claims of Kinfolk*; Konadu, *Akan Diaspora*; Rucker, *River Flows On*; Jason R. Young, *Rituals of Resistance*; Gomez, *Exchanging Our Country Marks*.

6. Mary Ridout to Anne Ogle, March 2, 1785, Ridout Family Papers, MdSA.
7. John Ridout Will, 1797, ibid.
8. Mary Ridout, Manumission Record for Charity Folks, December 6, 1797, AACCMR, 825:17–18.
9. Anne Ogle, Manumission Record for James, October 1789, AACCMR.
10. John Davidson, Manumission Record for Thomas Folks, 1794, Anne Arundel County Court, Land Records, MdSA.
11. John Ridout, Manumission Record for Harriet Jackson, 1786, in ibid. See also the lengthy codicil to the 1807 manumission record for Charity Folks (AACCMR, 830:2–6).
12. John Ridout, Manumission Record for Mary Folks, 1791, AACCMR. See also Mary Folks, Certificate of Freedom, 1811, Anne Arundel County Court, Certificates of Freedom, 823:8, MdSA.
13. Janice Hayes-Williams, conversation with author, November 1, 2009, Annapolis, Md.; Orlando Ridout IV, conversation with author, December 16, 2009, Annapolis, Md.
14. King, "Out of Bounds"; Schweninger, "Fragile Nature of Freedom."
15. Perbi, *History of Indigenous Slavery*, 4.
16. Gomez, *Exchanging Our Country Marks*, 14; see also 19–20, 168.
17. Penningroth, *Claims of Kinfolk*, 79–109.
18. Ibid., 1–12, 163–86.
19. Pargas, *Quarters and the Fields*, 202, 113.
20. William Cornish interview in Blassingame, *Slave Testimony*, 424–25.
21. *Memoir of Old Elizabeth*, 7.
22. Douglass, *Narrative*, 2.
23. Pargas, *Quarters and the Fields*; Grivno, *Gleanings of Freedom*; Berry, "Swing the Sickle."
24. S. Griffith to F. Garettson, n.d., Jay Family Papers, MS 1828, Maryland Historical Society.
25. Ibid.
26. Ibid.
27. John Davidson Daybook, March 4, 22, October 23, 1782, MdSA; John Davidson Account Book, December 10, 1785, Library of Congress.
28. See John Davidson Account Book; John Davidson Daybook. Born in Scotland, Davidson (1738–94) was claims comptroller of Annapolis and a partner in an import firm, Wallace, Davidson, and Johnson, established in 1771. In the 1790s, Davidson purchased what is now called Reynolds Tavern on Church Circle.
29. Condon, "Significance of Group Manumissions," 75.
30. Ibid., 77.
31. Ibid., 76.
32. Jennifer Hull Dorsey, *Hirelings*, 62.
33. Condon, "Significance of Group Manumissions," 76.
34. Jennifer Hull Dorsey, *Hirelings*, 62.
35. John Welch, Manumission Record for Susanna and Rachel Hawkins, February 1803, AACCMR, 825:132.
36. Schermerhorn, *Money over Mastery*, 22–62.
37. Dataset created by author.

38. Margaret (Mary) Callahan, Manumission Record for Rachel and Lucy, December 24, 1801, AACCMR, 825:101–2.
39. Margaret (Mary) Callahan, Manumission Record for William, Horace, and Rebecca, May 15, 1820, AACCMR, 831:172–73.
40. Joan C. Scurlock, "The Bishop Family of Annapolis," unpublished manuscript, 1999, 32, Banneker-Douglass Museum.
41. Rebecca Bishop, Certificate of Freedom, November 16, 1831, Anne Arundel County Court, Certificates of Freedom, 824:11; William S. Green, Manumission Record for William Bishop, June 6, 1822, AACCMR, 831:244.
42. William Bishop, Manumission Record for Horace Bishop, 1821, AACCMR, 831:172–73.
43. Mary Armiger, Manumission Record for Abigail, October 4, 1817, AACCMR, 831:60–61; Ann Munroe, Manumission Record for Fanny, July 29, 1818, AACCMR, 831:80–81.
44. William Johnson, Manumission Record for Cassandra Johnson and Her Three Children, August 14, 1822, AACCMR, 831:251.
45. Richard Mullin, Manumission Record for Susanna Mullin, Eliza Mullin, Hagar Mullin, and Priscilla Mullin, October 22, 1817, AACCMR, 831:132.
46. Elizabeth and Hester Hood, Manumission Record for Anna and Her Two Children, Eli and Washington; Cassy and Her Five Children, Pressy, Joshua, Henrietta, Peter, and Henry; Louisa and Her Children, William, Milly and Sally; Retty and Her Child, Jacob; Darkey and Her Children, George, Henry, and Henrietta; Vilet Susan and Her Children, Samuel and William; Jenny Hester and Her Children, Jerry, Mary, James, Dilly, Rebecca, and Richard; Sarah Eliza and her children, Elisha, Rosilla, Jane, and Anna; Norry and Her Two Children, Charlotte and Mary; and Negro Man John, January 6, 1823, AACCMR, 831:254–55.
47. Araminta Harrison, Manumission Record for Fanny and William, August 31, 1816, AACCMR, 831:7.
48. Eliza Hood, Manumission Record for Kitty Prout, March 19, 1823, AACCMR, 831:258–59.
49. Sam Gibson, Manumission Record for Patty Lee, January 12, 1811, AACCMR, 830:137.
50. Sam Gibson, Manumission Record for Anne Lee, April 2, 1811, AACCMR, 830:145–46; Sam Gibson, Manumission Record for Henry Lee, January 24, 1811, AACCMR, 830:146–47.
51. Catherine Hutton, Manumission Record for Juliet, January 25, 1830, AACCMR, 831:452.
52. Catherine Hutton, Manumission Record for Casey Ellen, William, and Jane, January 25, 1830, AACCMR, 831:450–51; Catherine Hutton, Manumission Record for Juliet, January 25, 1830, AACCMR, 831:452.
53. James Henry, Manumission Record for William, 1802, AACCMR, 25:129.
54. Benjamin Badger, Manumission Record for Hess, October 30, 1821, AACCMR, 831:216–17.
55. John Adams, Manumission Record for Rachel, Evina Anne, and John, November 21, 1818, AACCMR, 831:93.
56. George Johnson, Manumission Record for Mary and Her Children, 1801, AACCMR, 830:175.

57. Isaac and Mary Paul, Manumission Record for Philip and Mary Howard, June 29, 1818, AACCMR, 831:78–79; Philip Howard, Manumission Record for George and Ruth Howard, June 30, 1818, AACCMR, 831:76–77.

58. Horatio Ridout, Manumission Record for Susan and Sarah, March 18, 1828, AACCMR, 831:394–95.

59. William Reynolds, Manumission Record for Elizabeth and Her Children, November 17, 1804, AACCMR, 825:205–7.

60. Thomas Snowden, Manumission Record for Viney, June 9, 1829, AACCMR, 831:440–41; Thomas Snowden, Manumission Record for Ellen, Priscilla, and Peter, June 9, 1829, AACCMR, 831:441–44.

61. Caroline Hammond interview in Rawick, *American Slave*, 16:20.

62. Condon, "Significance of Group Manumissions," 79–80.

63. Perry Lewis interview in Rawick, *American Slave*, 16:49.

64. Joseph C. Dorsey, "Women without History."

65. Blake, *Memoirs of Margaret Jane Blake*, 8.

66. Ibid.

67. Mary Ridout, Manumission Record for Charity Folks and Others, August 1807, AACCMR, 830:2–6.

68. Penningroth, *Claims of Kinfolk*, 13–44.

69. U.S. Census, 1810; Janice Hayes-Williams, conversation with author, November 1, 2009, Annapolis, Md.

70. Heather Andrea Williams, *Help Me to Find My People*, 17.

Chapter 4. Moving Slavery, Shaping Freedom

1. Wesley, "Woman's Place," 59.

2. Mary Ridout, Manumission Record for Charity Folks and Others, August 1807, AACCMR, 830:2–6; Mary Ridout, Manumission Record for Charity Folks, December 6, 1797, AACCMR, 825:17–18.

3. Mary Ridout, Manumission Record for Charity Folks and Others, August 1807, AACCMR, 830:2–6.

4. Douglass, *My Bondage and My Freedom*, 51.

5. Bardaglio, *Reconstructing the Household*; Fox-Genovese, *Within the Plantation Household*; Glymph, *Out of the House*; Jennifer Hull Dorsey, *Hirelings*; Edwards, *People and Their Peace*.

6. Myers, *Forging Freedom*, 12.

7. Scott, *Degrees of Freedom*; Rockman, *Scraping By*; Nash, *Forging Freedom*; Berlin, *Slaves without Masters*; Windham, "Bondage, Bias, and the Bench"; Whitman, *Challenging Slavery in the Chesapeake*; Phillips, *Freedom's Port*; Brackett, *Negro in Maryland*; Whitman, *Price of Freedom*; Franklin, *Free Negro in North Carolina*; Adele Logan Alexander, *Ambiguous Lives*; Schwalm, *Hard Fight for We*; Leslie, *Woman of Color*.

8. Schweninger, "Property Owning Free African-American Women," 16.

9. King, *Essence of Liberty*, 60.

10. Whitman, "Manumission and Apprenticeship," 57.

11. Schweninger, *Black Property Owners*, 61–96.

12. Wallace, "Fair Daughters of Africa," 119.
13. Ham, *List of Free Black Heads of Families*, 8–15.
14. Jennifer Hull Dorsey, *Hirelings*, 77.
15. Phillips, *Freedom's Port*, especially 145–76.
16. King, "Out of Bounds."
17. Bardaglio, *Reconstructing the Household*; Edwards, "Marriage Covenant." See also Bleser, *In Joy and in Sorrow*.
18. Stevenson, *Life in Black and White*.
19. Rockman, *Scraping By*, 166.
20. U.S. Census, 1830–50; Janice Hayes-Williams, conversation with author, November 1, 2009, Annapolis, Md.
21. U.S. Census, 1810–40.
22. Baltimore City Directories, 1840–60, MdSA.
23. Hannah Murray Testimony, in *Lake v. Bishop*.
24. Rockman, *Scraping By*, 167.
25. Jennifer Hull Dorsey, *Hirelings*, 75.
26. Rockman, *Scraping By*, 167.
27. Dunbar, *Fragile Freedom*, 43.
28. Rockman, *Scraping By*, 166.
29. Jennifer Hull Dorsey, *Hirelings*, 74.
30. For an overview of this debate, see Stevenson, "Black Family Structure."
31. Lebsock, *Free Women of Petersburg*.
32. Margaret Mercer, Manumission Record for Nelly Sparrow, October 26, 1833, AACCMR, 831:553–54.
33. James Jackson Testimony, in *Lake v. Bishop*. For general discussions of enslaved fathers, see Ball, *Slavery in the United States*; Green, *Narrative of Events*; Blake, *Memoirs of Margaret Jane Blake*; Pennington, *Fugitive Blacksmith*; John Thompson, *Life of John Thompson*; Ward, *Autobiography of a Fugitive Negro*.
34. James Jackson Testimony.
35. Randolph Latimer Brandt, Manumission Record for Benjamin, April 27, 1805, AACCMR, 825:228–29.
36. Jennifer Hull Dorsey, *Hirelings*, 62.
37. Ham, "Role of African American Women," 370.
38. Tyler-McGraw, *African Republic*, 8.
39. John Russwurm, *Freedom's Journal*, March 14, 1829; Tyler-McGraw, *African Republic*, 2. Russwurm's pieces in *Freedom's Journal* illustrate his evolution from an antiemigrationist to a supporter of the effort. See also Eslinger, "Brief Career of Rufus F. Bailey"; Beyan, *African American Settlements*; James, *Struggles of John Brown Russwurm*.
40. James Hall, "An Address to the Free People of Color of the State of Maryland," Baltimore, December 1858, American Pamphlets Collection, Library of Congress.
41. Beyan, *African American Settlements*, 35.
42. *Freedom's Journal*, November 2, 1827.
43. Walker, "David Walker's Appeal," 84, 85.
44. Saillant, "Black Body Erotic," 405–6.
45. Mitchell, *Righteous Propagation*, 21; Brugger, *Maryland*, 213.

90   NOTES TO CHAPTER FOUR

46. James Jackson Testimony, in *Lake v. Bishop*.
47. Ibid.
48. Ibid.
49. Hannah Murray Testimony, in *Lake v. Bishop*.
50. *Lake v. Bishop*.
51. See Mary Folks, Hannah Murray, James Jackson, and Stephen Rummels Testimony, all in *Lake v. Bishop*.
52. Hannah Murray Testimony.
53. Mary Ridout to Anne Ogle, 1797, Ridout Family Papers, MdSA.
54. Horatio Ridout and Samuel Ridout, Bond, 1797, Anne Arundel County Court, Chancery Papers, MdSA.
55. Mary Ridout to Anne Ogle, 1797, Ridout Family Papers.
56. Ibid., December 1807.
57. "The Estate of Mary Owings, 1835," Dr. John Ridout Account Book, Dr. John Ridout Papers, MdSA.
58. Rockman, "Women's Labor."
59. Schweninger, *Black Property Owners*, 108–9.
60. Stevenson, *Life in Black and White*, 162. According to Stevenson, in Loudoun County, Virginia, the "racial hierarchy placed free persons of color outside sanctioned boundaries of southern society."
61. John Ridgley paid Hercules wages from 1830 to 1851 ("Hercules," Kent Lancaster Papers, HNHS).
62. Brackett, *Negro in Maryland*, 188; Schweninger, *Black Property Owners*, 64.
63. Brackett, *Negro in Maryland*, 188.
64. Jennifer Hull Dorsey, *Hirelings*, 83.
65. Schweninger, *Black Property Owners*, 131.
66. Baltimore City Directory, 1830, MdSA.
67. Calderhead, "Anne Arundel Blacks."
68. "Estate of Mary Owings, 1835."
69. Michael P. Johnson and Roark, *Black Masters*.
70. Calderhead, "Anne Arundel Blacks," 18. Bishop and his children rented out property on the present-day site of the city courthouse. See *Maryland Gazette*, 1840–50; Leone, *Archaeology of Liberty*.
71. Edward Boothe, Manumission Record for Edward Boothe, 1816, AACCMR, 830:339.
72. Koger, *Black Slaveowners*; Woodson, *Free Negro Owners*; Michael P. Johnson and Roark, *Black Masters*.
73. Schweninger, *Black Property Owners*, 111.
74. Thomas Folks, Manumission Record for Samuel Heywood, January 11, 1804, AACCMR, 825:167–68; U.S. Census, 1820.
75. U.S. Census, 1830.
76. Ibid., 1830, 1840.
77. Woodson, *Free Negro Owners*, 16.
78. "List of Insolvent Debtors," *Maryland Gazette*, January 1805. See also Act Relating to Insolvent Debtors, 1804 Session Laws, Archives of Maryland Online, http://aomol.msa.maryland.gov/000001/000562/html/am562—2.html.

79. Charity Folks Will, 1828, quoted in *Lake v. Bishop*; Charity Folks, Last Will and Testament, 1828, AACCRW.
80. Dr. John Ridout Testimony, in *Lake v. Bishop*.
81. Charity Folks, Last Will and Testament, 1828, AACCRW.
82. Ibid.
83. Calderhead, "Anne Arundel Blacks," 18–19.
84. 1880 Annapolis Real Estate Assessment, Annapolis Mayor and Aldermen, Assessment Record, MdSA.
85. William Bishop and Charity Bishop to Dr. John Ridout, Deed, 1870, Dr. William Bishop Papers/Doris Moses Collection, MdSA.
86. Orlando Ridout IV, interview with author, December 16, 2010, Annapolis, Md.
87. Berlin, *Slaves without Masters*, 57.
88. Painter, "Soul Murder and Slavery."
89. See Franklin, *Free Negro in North Carolina*; Berlin, *Slaves without Masters*.
90. Jennifer Hull Dorsey, "Free People of Color." See also Jennifer Hull Dorsey, *Hirelings*.
91. Brugger, *Maryland*, 170.
92. Kilty, *Index to the Laws of Maryland*, 597.
93. Ibid., 838.
94. Jennifer Hull Dorsey, *Hirelings*, 31.
95. Dataset created by author; AACCRW; Baltimore County Court, Register of Wills, MdSA. Apprenticeships granted to whites and blacks were surveyed from 1770 to 1830. Indentures featuring African Americans began appearing in greater numbers after 1812. At the outset, an equal number of black male indenture certificates were chosen to provide an even dataset. However, it became apparent this would present a skewed database, implying that an equal number of African American males and females served as apprentices. Thus, this sample includes a portion of indentures referencing all black women and some black men from 1790 to 1830 in both counties.
96. Whitman, "Manumission and Apprenticeship," 66.
97. Jennifer Hull Dorsey, *Hirelings*, 82–99.
98. Dataset created by author. See, for example, An Act Authorizing the Judges of the Orphans Court to Bind out the Children of Free Negroes and Mulattoes, Laws of Maryland—1818, Chap. 189, Archives of Maryland Online, http://msa.maryland.gov/megafile/msa/speccol/sc2900/sc2908/000001/000141/html/am141—697.html.
99. Dataset created by author; AACCRW; Baltimore County Court, Register of Wills (Indentures), MdSA.
100. Kinsey Johns and Johns John, Petition for Clem, 1806, Baltimore County Petitions and Orders, Schweninger Collection, MSA SC 4239-14-31, MdSA; Kinsey Johns and Johns John, Petition for Clem, 1807, Baltimore County Petitions and Orders, Schweninger Collection, MSA SC 4239-14-32, MdSA.
101. Kinsey Johns and Johns John, Petition for Clem, 1807.
102. John Wright, Apprenticeship Deed for George Barrows, Baltimore County Court, Petitions and Orders, MdSA.
103. Charles Mahoney, Apprenticeship Deed for Amos Yealdhall, 1805, Certificates of Indenture, AACCRW; Charles Mahoney, Apprenticeship Deed for Amos Yealdhall, 1805,

Baltimore County Court, Register of Wills (Indentures), MdSA; Charles Mahoney, Apprenticeship Deed for Daniel Yealdhall, 1816, Certificates of Indenture, AACCRW; Charles Mahoney, Apprenticeship Deed for Thomas Yealdhall, 1823, Certificates of Indenture, AACCRW.

104. Dataset created by author. See also Negro Catherine, Apprenticeship Deed for Children, Baltimore County Court, Register of Wills (Indentures), MdSA.

105. Alexander Jaquin, Apprenticeship Deed for Catherine Jones, September 1, 1824, AACCRW.

106. Albert Bantan, Apprenticeship Deed for Maria Toogood, August 8, 1826, AACCRW.

107. Benjamin Faulkner, Apprenticeship Deed for Bope, 1826, AACCRW.

108. Edward Norris, Apprenticeship Deed for Solomon Johnson, 1814, Baltimore County Orphans' Court, Proceedings, MdSA.

109. William Hink, Apprenticeship Deed for Samuel, 1819, AACCRW.

110. Horace Bishop, Apprenticeship Deed, 1823, AACCRW.

111. Moses Bishop, Apprenticeship Deed, 1850, AACCRW.

112. Whitman, *Price of Freedom*, 25–31.

113. Carr, "Development," 56.

114. Baltimore City Trustees of the Poor, Relief and Welfare Rolls, 1832–36, 1840–42, 1865–66, MdSA.

115. Daniels, "WANTED"; Zipf, "Reconstructing 'Free Woman.'"

116. Roberts, "Welfare."

117. Roberts, *Killing the Black Body*, 294.

Conclusion. Memorials and Reparations by the Living

1. Testimony of Hannah Murray, in *Lake v. Bishop*.

2. Ibid. The house was not William Bishop's but in fact was purchased by Charity Bishop and her sister, Mary Folks, in 1816 (Shackel and Little, *Historical Archaeology of the Chesapeake*, 201; Calderhead, "Slavery in Maryland," 308; Calderhead, "Anne Arundel Blacks," 18; Mullins, *Race and Affluence*; U.S. Census, 1830).

3. Testimony of Hannah Murray, in *Lake v. Bishop*.

4. Family tree, Ennis and Minsky Families of Annapolis, Doris Moses Collection, MdSA.

5. Bishop family genealogy chart, Dr. William Bishop Papers/Doris Moses Collection, MdSA.

6. "About BDM," Banneker-Douglass Museum Website, http://www.bdmuseum.com/index.html.

7. Christian Davenport, "Roots of Reconciliation," *Washington Post*, September 30, 2004.

8. See Kunta Kinte–Alex Haley Foundation Website, http://www.kintehaley.org/foundationmission.html.

9. See "The Original Plaque," Kunta Kinte–Alex Haley Foundation Website, http://www.kintehaley.org/memorialelements.html#plaque.

10. Orlando Ridout IV, conversation with author, December 16, 2009, Annapolis, Md.

11. Maryland General Assembly, Senate, "A Senate Joint Resolution Concerning Slavery in Maryland," S. J. Res. 6.2007, February 16, 2007; House Joint Resolution 4, 71R3168, February 23, 2007. For the text of the resolution, see Session Laws, 2007, Archives of Maryland Online, http://aomol.MdSA.maryland.gov/megafile/MdSA/speccol/sc2900/sc2908/000001/000803/html/am803—4094.html.

12. City Council of the City of Annapolis, Resolution R-17-07, May 5, 2007, http://www.ci.annapolis.md.us/docs/default-source/legislation/r-59-11-amended-annapolis-commission-on-maryland-s-constitution-of-1864-and-the-abolishment-of-slavery.pdf?sfvrsn=4.

13. Jenna Johnson, "Students Trace University's Ties to Slavery," *Washington Post*, October 10, 2009; University of Maryland, College Park, News Release, "Release of New Study on Slavery and UM's Early History," October 9, 2009, http://www.newsdesk.umd.edu/sociss/release.cfm?ArticleID=1991; *Washington Informer*, October 29, 2009. Brown University and other institutions of higher education have acknowledged their participation in the Atlantic slave trade, and the connections between universities and slavery were explored at a conference, Slavery and the University: Histories and Legacies, hosted by Emory University, February 3–5, 2011.

14. See "About Us: The Organization," National Underground Railroad Freedom Center, http://www.freedomcenter.org/about-us/.

15. Wilder, "U.S. National Slavery Museum."

16. Calderhead, "Anne Arundel Blacks," 18.

17. Annapolis City Directories, 1860–90, Blacks in Annapolis Project, MdSA, http://www.mdslavery.net/s_annapolis/electronic.html.

18. Joan C. Scurlock, "The Bishop Family of Annapolis," unpublished manuscript, 1999, 87, Banneker-Douglass Museum.

19. Calderhead, "Anne Arundel Blacks," 18.

20. Scurlock, "Bishop Family of Annapolis," 21.

21. Hansen, *Reaching Out*, 57.

22. Ibid.; "Rev. Shelton Hale Bishop Dies," *New York Times*, August 25, 1962.

23. Bishop, "History of St. Philip's Church"; Hansen, *Reaching Out*, 36–37.

24. Some two hundred families lived in the apartments on West 135th street between Seventh and Lenox Avenue where the Harlem YMCA now stands. Both the apartments and the YMCA established by Bishop and Nail were awarded landmark status in the late twentieth century (Hansen, *Reaching Out*, 36–37; "History," St. Philip's Website, http://www.stphilipsharlem.org/history).

25. "Deed of Property, 1910," container 38, St. Philip's Episcopal Church Collection, Schomburg Center for Research in Black Culture, New York Public Library.

26. Hansen, *Reaching Out*, 38–39.

27. Ibid., 53; "Rev. Shelton Hale Bishop Dies," *New York Times*, August 25, 1962.

28. Elizabeth Bishop Davis Trussell obituary, *New York Times*, February 4, 2010; Professional Papers, Elizabeth B. Davis Collection, Schomburg Center for Research in Black Culture, New York Public Library.

BIBLIOGRAPHY

Primary Sources
UNPUBLISHED MANUSCRIPTS

Baltimore City Archives, Baltimore
Court Records of Baltimore City, 1729–1830
Early Records of Baltimore, vols. 1 and 2
Ordinances and Resolutions of the Mayor of Baltimore
Tax Assessor Notebooks

Banneker-Douglass Museum, Annapolis, Md.
Joan C. Scurlock, "The Bishop Family of Annapolis," Unpublished Manuscript, 1999

British Library, London
Correspondence of Thomas Pitt, Additional Misc. Papers
Misc. Papers Referring to American Affairs, 1718–1796
Treasury Papers, Misc.

City Museums of Bowie, Bowie, Md.
Ogle Family Estate Inventories and Wills

David Library of the American Revolution, Washington Crossing, Pa.
Sol Feinstein Collection
Mordecai Gist Papers

Family History Library, Salt Lake City, Utah
Anne Arundel County Court, Guardian Accounts, 1833–1853
Anne Arundel County Court Records, Administrative Accounts, 1785–1840
Anne Arundel County Court Records, Bonds and Deeds, 1777–1860
Kent County Court, Administrative Bonds, 1740–1789
Kent County Court, Bonds, 1664–1789
Kent County Court, Land Records, 1782–1790
Kent County Register of Wills—Inventories, 1788–1795
Maryland Miscellaneous Court Records
Miscellaneous American Revolution Records

Prince George's County Land Records, 1696–1884
Prince George's County Probate Records, 1703–1858

Hampton National Historic Site, Baltimore
John Edgar Howard Family Papers
Kent Lancaster Papers
Ridgely Family Papers
John (III) and Lillian Ketcham Ridgely Papers
G. Howard and Gene L. White Papers
Henry White Family Papers

NEWSPAPER COLLECTION
Boston Recorder and Religious Telegraph
The Telescope

Johns Hopkins University, Baltimore
James Birney Collection
Carroll Collection
Howard-Ridgely-Maynard Family Papers
Merchant Records
Merryman and Crane Family Papers
Weatherburn Family Papers

Lovely Lane United Methodist Church Museum and Archive, Baltimore
Baltimore Conference Records
Baltimore Conference Stewardship Books, 1770–1815
Chalmers-Roszel Correspondence

LOCAL CHURCH HISTORY COLLECTION
Baltimore North: Sharp Street Vertical File

Library of Congress, Washington, D.C.
Carroll Family Papers
Carter Family Papers
Church Family Papers
John Davidson Account Book
Gabriel Duvall Papers, 1765–1920
William Ennals Papers, vol. 1, 1771–1774
Peter Force Collection
Galloway-Maxcy-Markhoe Family Papers
Thomas Haskins Papers
Robert Honeyman Diary
Huie, Reid, and Company Papers, 1784–1796
Joshua Johnson Letterbook, 1785–1788
Thomas Sim Lee Papers, 1771–1780
Maryland Intendant of the Revolution Letterbook (Daniel St. Thomas), 1785–1787

Maryland Miscellany, 1632–1936
Maryland Salt Works Papers, 1770–1811
Charles Carnan Ridgley Account Book

Maryland Historical Society, Baltimore
Joseph Sweetman Aimes Collection
Baltimore City and County Trustees of the Poor, Relief and Welfare Rolls
Baltimore County Court, Chattel Records, 1773–1784
Charles Carroll of Carrollton Papers
Robert Carter Letterbooks
Robert Carter Papers
Chapman Family Papers
Cheston-Galloway Papers
Chew Family Papers
Cockey Family Papers
Dorsey Family Papers
Dulany Family Papers
Jacob Franklin Accounts
Giddings Family Papers
John Hanson Ledger
John Hanson Papers
Robert Goodloe Harper Family Papers
Hoffman Family Papers
Samuel Gover Hopkins Collection
Howard Family Papers
J. E. Howard Estate Papers
John Howard Estate Papers
Jay Family Papers
Serene Johnson Collection
Jones Family Papers
Francis Scott Key Papers
Maryland Colonization Society Papers
William Patterson Account Books
Principio Company Papers
Quaker Church Records
Revolutionary War Collection
Captain Charles Ridgely Family Papers
Ridgely Family Papers
Ridgely Land Papers
Ridgely-Pue Papers
Thomas Rutland Letterbook
Thomas Rutledge Letterbook
Slavery, Misc., 17th Century
Tilghman/Lloyd Family Papers
W. Emerson Wilson Collection

Maryland State Archives, Annapolis

SPECIAL COLLECTIONS

Dr. William Bishop Papers/Doris Moses Collection
John Davidson Daybook, 1781–1782
Farmer's National Bank
Ridout Family Bible
Ridout Family Papers
Dr. John Ridout Papers
Mary Ogle Ridout Papers
St. Anne's Parish Records
Savings Bank of Baltimore Records (Journal), 1818–1827
Tayloe Family Bible

GOVERNMENT DOCUMENTS

Alleghany County Court, Equity Papers, 1815–1828
Annapolis Mayor and Aldermen, Assessment Record, 1880
Anne Arundel County, Federal Direct Tax List, 1798
Anne Arundel County Almshouse, Records, 1820–1870
Anne Arundel County Court, Certificates of Freedom, 1810–1864
Anne Arundel County Court, Chancery Papers, 1790–1835
Anne Arundel County Court, Chattel Records, 1829–1851
Anne Arundel County Court, Estate Inventories, 1750–1840
Anne Arundel County Court, Equity Papers, 1851–1852
Anne Arundel County Court, Judgment Records, 1768–1770
Anne Arundel County Court, Land Records, 1653–1844
Anne Arundel County Court, Manumission Records, 1785–1865
Anne Arundel County Court, Petitions and Orders, 1814–1820
Anne Arundel County Court, Register of Wills (Indentures), 1779–1846
Anne Arundel County Orphans' Court, Docket, 1771–1784
Anne Arundel County Orphans' Court, Proceedings, 1784–1815
Baltimore City, Trustees of the Poor Proceedings, 1833–1842
Baltimore County Court, Certificates of Freedom, 1806–1816, 1830
Baltimore County Court, Chattel Records, 1760–1814
Baltimore County Court, Marriage Records, 1815–1832
Baltimore County Court, Petitions and Orders
Baltimore County Court, Register of Wills, 1770–1830
Baltimore County Court, Register of Wills (Indentures), 1794–1780
Baltimore County Court, Renunciations, 1825–1848
Baltimore County Orphans' Court, Proceedings, 1790–1890
Frederick County Court, Petitions, 1828
General Court of the Western Shore, Judgment Record, 1778
General Court of the Western Shore, Minutes of the Proceedings
Hartford County Court, Manumission Records, 1774–1784
Maryland Census, 1776, 1778

Maryland Convention, Proceedings, 1775–1782
Maryland Council of Public Safety, Journal, 1770–1790
Maryland Council of Public Safety, Papers, 1775–1782
Maryland Penitentiary, Records
Maryland Prerogative Court, Records (Testamentary), 1768–1770
Maryland State Papers, General Assembly Papers, 1775–1789
Maryland State Papers, Black Books
Maryland State Papers, Blue Books
Maryland State Papers, Brown Books
Maryland State Papers, Red Books
Maryland State Papers, Revolutionary War Collection
Prince George's County Court, Black Papers, 1780–1860
Prince George's County Court, Certificates of Freedom, 1760–1830
Prince George's County Court, Estate Inventories, 1750–1830
Prince George's County Court, Freedom Affidavits, 1810–1850
Prince George's County Court, Docket and Minutes Book, September 1810–April 1811
Schweninger Collection
Talbot County, Freedom Certificates, 1806–1860
Talbot County Circuit Court, Petitions, 1803–1882

Public Records Office, Kew, Richmond, uk

Papers of the American Loyalist Claims Commission
Committee on the Black Poor
Wills and Death Duties, 1740–1830

National Archives, Washington, D.C.

Civil War Pension Records
U.S. Federal Census, 1790–1870

Virginia Historical Society, Richmond

Carter Family Papers
Robert Carter Papers
Faulkner Family Papers
Hunter Family Papers
Mercer Family Papers
John Fenton Mercer Letterbook
Anne Tasker Ogle Papers

Schomburg Center for Research in Black Culture, New York Public Library, New York

Shelton Hale Bishop Collection
George Bragg Collection
Alex Haley Papers
St. Philip's Episcopal Church Records
Elizabeth Bishop Davis Trussell Papers

Southern Baptist Historical Library and Archives, Nashville, Tenn.
First Baptist Church of Baltimore, 1773–1968
Gunpowder Baptist Church, Maryland, 1860–1933, 1940–1966
Lower Dublin Baptist Church, Pennsylvania, 1862–1869

St. Philip's Episcopal Church, New York
Miscellaneous Papers

University of California, Santa Barbara
Religious Leaders of America Collection

NEWSPAPERS

Afro-American
Baltimore Daily Intelligencer
Baltimore Evening Post
Baltimore Sun Times
Gazette of the United States
Genius of Universal Emancipation and Baltimore Courier
Herald of Liberty
Maryland Gazette
Maryland Journal and Baltimore Advertiser
Niles Register
Spectator
Washington Post

Selected Digital and Published Primary Sources
INTERNET DATABASES AND RESEARCH COLLECTIONS

AfriGeneas (http://www.afrigeneas.com/slavedata/)
Ancestry.com (www.ancestry.com)
Archaeology in Annapolis Project (http://www.aia.umd.edu/)
Archives of Maryland Online (http://www.aomol.net/html/index.html)
Belair at Bowie: Flight to Freedom (http://www.mdslavery.net/bowie/database.html)
Blacks in Annapolis (http://www.mdslavery.net/blacks_annapolis/intro.html)
Documenting the American South (http://docsouth.unc.edu)
Liberian Repatriates (http://www.liberianrepatriates.com/)
Race and Slavery (Proquest History Vault)
Slave Trade Database (http://www.slavevoyages.org/tast/index.faces)
UNESCO Slave Trade Route Project (http://www.unesco.org/new/en/culture/themes/dialogue/the-slave-route/)
University of Virginia Historical Census Browser (http://mapserver.lib.virginia.edu/)

PUBLISHED PRIMARY SOURCES

Ball, Charles. *Slavery in the United States: A Narrative of the Life and Adventures of Charles Ball, a Black Man.* Detroit: Negro History Press, 1970.

Barnes, Robert, ed. *Baltimore Town and Fells Point Directory of 1796–1803.* Silver Spring, Md.: Family Line, 1983.

Berlin, Ira, and Leslie S. Rowland, eds. *Families and Freedom: A Documentary History of African American Kinship in the Civil War Era.* New York: New Press, 1990.

Blackford, John. *Ferry Hill Plantation Journal, January 4, 1838–January 15, 1839.* Ed. Fletcher M. Green. Chapel Hill: University of North Carolina Press, 1961.

Blake, Margaret Jane. *Memoirs of Margaret Jane Blake of Baltimore, MD and Selections in Prose and Verse.* Ed. Sarah R. Levering. Philadelphia: Innes, 1830. Electronic ed. University of North Carolina at Chapel Hill, 1999.

Blassingame, John, ed. *Slave Testimony: Two Centuries of Letters, Speeches, Interviews, and Autobiographies.* Baton Rouge: Louisiana State University Press, 1977.

Bond, Scott. *From Slavery to Wealth: The Life of Scott Bond, Fayetteville.* Ed. Willard B. Gatewood. 1917; Fayetteville, Ark.: Phoenix, 2008.

Botkin, R. A., ed. *Lay My Burden Down: A Folk History of Slavery.* Chicago: University of Chicago Press, 1945.

Calvert, Rosalie Stier. *Rosalie Stier Calvert, Mistress of Riversdale: The Plantation Letters of Rosalie Stier Calvert, 1795–1821.* Ed. Margaret Law Callcott. Baltimore: Johns Hopkins University Press, 1991.

Carothers, Bettie Sterling. *1776 Census of Maryland.* 2nd ed. Decorah, Iowa: Anundsen, 1986.

Carroll, Charles. *Dear Papa, Dear Charley: The Papers of Charles Carroll of Carrollton.* Ed. Ronald Hoffman, Sally D. Mason, and Eleanor Darcy. Chapel Hill: University of North Carolina Press for the Omohundro Institute of Early American History Culture, the Maryland Historical Society, and the Maryland State Archives, 2001.

Catterall, Helen Tunnicliff, ed. *Judicial Cases Concerning American Slavery and the Negro.* Vol. 4. Washington, D.C.: Carnegie Institute of Washington, D.C., 1936.

Clark, Walter, and William Saunders, eds. *The State Records of North Carolina.* Vol. 1. New York: AMS, 1968.

Clayton, Ralph. *Slavery, Slaveholding, and the Free Black Population of Antebellum Baltimore.* Bowie, Md.: Heritage, 2005.

Coker, Daniel. *The Journal of Daniel Coker.* Baltimore: Coale, 1830. Electronic ed. University of North Carolina at Chapel Hill, 2000.

Cooper, Ezekiel. *Beams of Light on Early Methodism in America.* New York: Phillips, Hunt, Cranston, and Stowe, 1887. Electronic ed. University of North Carolina at Chapel Hill, 2000.

Crèvecoeur, J. Hector St. Jean. *Letters from an American Farmer.* New York: Duffield, 1904.

Curtin, Philip, ed. *Africa Remembered: Narratives by West Africans from the Era of the Slave Trade.* Madison: University of Wisconsin Press, 1967.

Donnan, Elizabeth, ed. *Documents Illustrative of the History of the Slave Trade to America.* New York: Octagon, 1969.

BIBLIOGRAPHY

Douglass, Frederick. *My Bondage and My Freedom*. Ed. William L. Andrews. Urbana: University of Illinois Press, 1992.

———. *Narrative of the Life of Frederick Douglass*. In *Classic Slave Narratives*, ed. Henry Louis Gates Jr., 253–331. New York: Penguin, 1987.

Eddis, William. *Letters from America*. Ed. Aubrey C. Land. Cambridge: Harvard University Press, 1969.

Eltis, David, Stephen D. Behrendt, David Richardson, and Herbert S. Klein, eds. *The Trans-Atlantic Slave Trade: A Database on CD-ROM*. New York: Cambridge University Press, 1999.

Equiano, Olaudah. *The Life of Olaudah Equiano or Gustava Vassa, Written by Himself*. In *The Classic Slave Narratives*, ed. Henry Louis Gates Jr., 1–182. New York: Penguin, 1987.

Force, Peter, ed. *American Archives: A Documentary History of the American Colonies*. Vol. 4. Washington, D.C.: Library of Congress, 1937.

Goings, Henry. *Rambles of a Runaway from Southern Slavery*. Ed. Calvin Schermerhorn, Michael Plunkett, and Edward Gaynor. Charlottesville: University of Virginia Press, 2012.

Green, William. *Narrative of Events in the Life of William Green*. Springfield, Mass.: Guernsey, 1853. Electronic ed. University of North Carolina at Chapel Hill, 2000.

Grimké, Charlotte Forten. *The Journals of Charlotte Forten Grimké*. Ed. Brenda Stevenson. New York: Oxford University Press, 1988.

Ham, Deborah Newman. *List of Free Black Heads of Families in the First Census of the United States, 1790*. Washington, D.C.: National Archives and Records Service, 1973.

Hening, William. *The Statutes at Large; Being a Collection of All the Laws of Virginia, from the First Session of the Legislature in the Year 1619*. 1819; Charlottesville: University Press of Virginia for the Jamestown Foundation, 1969.

Hynson, Jerry M. *Maryland Freedom Papers: Anne Arundel County*. Westminster, Md.: Willow Bend, 2000.

Kilty, William. *Index to the Laws of Maryland: From the Year 1818 to 1825*. Annapolis, Md.: Hughes, 1827.

Lerner, Gerda, ed. *Black Women in White America: A Documentary History*. New York: Vintage, 1972.

Mellon, James. *Bullwhip Days: The Slaves Remember*. New York: Random House, 1974.

Memoir of Old Elizabeth, a Coloured Woman. Philadelphia: Collins, 1863. Electronic ed. University of North Carolina at Chapel Hill, 1999.

Minutes of the Methodist Conferences, Annually Held in America: From 1773–1813, Inclusive. New York: Hitt and Ware, 1813.

Papers of the Continental Congress. Washington, D.C.: National Archives and Records Service, 1971.

Peden, Henry C., Jr. *Inhabitants of Baltimore County, 1763–1774*. Westminster, Md.: Family Line, 1989.

———. *Quaker Records of Northern Maryland: Births, Deaths, Marriages and Abstracts from the Minutes, 1716–1800*. Westminster, Md.: Family Line, 1994.

Pennington, James W. C. *The Fugitive Blacksmith; or, Events in the History of James W. C. Pennington*. 3rd ed. Westport, Conn.: Negro Universities Press, 1971.

Piet, Mary A., and Stanley G. Piet, comps. *Early Catholic Church Records in Baltimore, Maryland, 1782 through 1800*. Westminster, Md.: Family Line, 1989.

Rawick, George P., ed. *The American Slave: A Composite Autobiography*. Vol. 16, Kansas, Kentucky, Maryland, Ohio, and Tennessee Narratives. Westport, Conn.: Greenwood, 1972.

———, ed. *The American Slave: A Composite Autobiography*. Supplemental ser. 2, vol. 1. Westport, Conn.: Greenwood, 1979.

Ripley, Peter C., ed. *The Black Abolitionist Papers: The United States, 1830–1846*. Vol. 3. Chapel Hill: University of North Carolina Press, 1991.

Rose, Willie Lee, ed. *A Documentary History of Slavery in North America*. Athens: University of Georgia Press, 1999.

Rothman, David, ed. *The Almshouse Experience: Collected Reports*. New York: Arno, 1827.

Schweninger, Loren, ed. *Race, Slavery, and Free Blacks*. Ser. 1, *Petitions to Southern Legislatures, 1777–1867*. Bethesda, Md.: University Publications of America, 1999.

———, ed. The *Southern Debate over Slavery*. Vol. 2, *Petitions to Southern County Courts, 1775–1867*. Urbana: University of Illinois Press, 2008.

Semmes, Raphael, ed. *Baltimore as Seen by Visitors*. Baltimore: Maryland Historical Society, 1953.

Sernett, Milton C. *Afro-American Religious History: A Documentary Witness*. Durham: Duke University Press, 1978.

Stampp, Kenneth, ed. *Records of Southern Plantations from the American Revolution to the Antebellum Period*. Frederick, Md.: University Publications of America, 1985.

Sterling, Dorothy, ed. *We Are Your Sisters: Black Women in the Nineteenth Century*. New York: Norton, 1997.

Still, William, ed. *The Underground Railroad: A Record of Facts, Authentic Narratives, Letters, Etc.* Chicago: Johnson, 1970.

Thompson, John. *The Life of John Thompson, a Fugitive Slave; Containing His History of 25 Years in Bondage and His Providential Escape*. Worcester: Thompson, 1856. Electronic ed. University of North Carolina at Chapel Hill, 1999.

Walker, David. "David Walker's Appeal." In *Crossing the Danger Water: Three Hundred Years of African-American Writing*, ed. Deirdre Mullane, 76–85. New York: Anchor, 1993.

Ward, Samuel Ringgold. *Autobiography of a Fugitive Negro: His Anti-Slavery Labours in the United States, Canada, and England*. London: Snow, 1855. Electronic ed. University of North Carolina at Chapel Hill, 1999.

Windley, Lathan A., comp. *Runaway Slave Advertisements: A Documentary History From the 1730s to 1790*. Vol. 2, *Maryland*. Westport, Conn.: Greenwood, 1983.

Secondary Sources

Adams, Catherine, and Elizabeth H. Pleck. *Love of Freedom: Black Women in Colonial and Revolutionary New England*. Oxford: Oxford University Press, 2010.

Alexander, Adele Logan. *Ambiguous Lives: Free Women of Color in Rural Georgia, 1789–1879*. Fayetteville: University of Arkansas Press, 1991.

———. *Homelands and Waterways: The American Journey of the Bond Family, 1846–1926.* New York: Pantheon, 1999.

———. *Parallel Worlds: The Remarkable Gibbs-Hunts and the Enduring (In)Significance of Melanin.* Charlottesville: University of Virginia Press, 2010.

Alexander, Leslie. "The Challenge of Race: Rethinking the Position of Black Women in the Field of Women's History." *Journal of Women's History* 16, no. 4 (2004): 50–60.

Altink, Henrice. *Representations of Slave Women in Discourses on Slavery and Abolition, 1780–1838.* New York: Routledge, 2007.

Bailey, Anne. *African Voices and the Transatlantic Slave Trade.* Boston: Beacon, 2005.

Baltz, Shirley. *Belair from the Beginning.* Bowie, Md.: City of Bowie Museums, 2005.

Baptist, Edward E. "'Cuffy,' 'Fancy Maids,' and 'One-Eyed Men': Rape, Commodification, and the Domestic Slave Trade in the United States." *American Historical Review* 106, no. 5 (2001): 1619–50.

Bardaglio, Peter Winthrop. *Reconstructing the Household: Families, Sex, and the Law in the Nineteenth-Century South.* Chapel Hill: University of North Carolina Press, 1995.

Bascom, William Russell. *Shango in the New World.* Austin: African and Afro-American Research Institute, University of Texas at Austin, 1972.

Berlin, Ira. *Many Thousands Gone: The First Two Centuries of Slavery in North America.* Cambridge: Belknap Press of Harvard University Press, 1998.

———. *Slaves without Masters: The Free Negro in the Antebellum South.* New York: Pantheon, 1975.

Berlin, Ira, and Philip D. Morgan, eds. *Cultivation and Culture: Labor and the Shaping of Slave Life in the Americas.* Charlottesville: University Press of Virginia, 1993.

Berry, Daina Ramey. *"Swing the Sickle for the Harvest Is Ripe": Gender and Slavery in Antebellum Georgia.* Urbana: University of Illinois Press, 2007.

———. "'We Sho Was Dressed Up': Slave Women, Material Culture, and Decorative Arts in Wilkes County, Georgia." In *The Savannah River Valley up to 1865: Fine Arts, Architecture, and Decorative Arts,* ed. Ashley Callahan, 73–83. Athens: Georgia Museum of Art, 2003.

Beyan, Amos. *African American Settlements in West Africa: John Brown Russwurm and the American Civilizing Efforts.* New York: Palgrave Macmillan, 2005.

Bezís-Selfa, John. *Forging America: Ironworkers, Adventurers, and the Industrious Revolution.* Ithaca: Cornell University Press, 2004.

Bishop, Shelton Hale. "A History of St. Philip's Church, New York City." *Historical Magazine of the Protestant Episcopal Church* 15 (1946): 298–317.

Blackett, R. J. M. *Beating against the Barriers: Biographical Essays in Nineteenth-Century Afro-American History.* Baton Rouge: Louisiana State University Press, 1986.

Blassingame, John. *The Slave Community: Plantation Life in the Antebellum South.* New York: Oxford University Press, 1972.

Bleser, Carol, ed. *In Joy and in Sorrow: Women, Family, and Marriage in the Victorian South, 1830–1900.* New York: Oxford University Press, 1991.

Block, Sharon. *Rape and Sexual Power in Early America.* Chapel Hill: University of North Carolina Press, 2006.

Boris, Eileen. "From Gender to Racialized Gender: Laboring Bodies That Matter." *International Labor and Working-Class History* 63 (2003): 9–13.

Brackett, Jeffrey R. *The Negro in Maryland: a Study of the Institution of Slavery*. 1889; Freeport, N.Y.: Books for Libraries, 1969.
Bradford, James C., ed. *Anne Arundel County, Maryland: A Bicentennial History, 1649–1977*. Annapolis: Anne Arundel County and Annapolis Bicentennial Committee, 1977.
Brana-Shute, Rosemary, and Randy J. Sparks, eds. *Paths to Freedom: Manumission in the Atlantic World*. Columbia: University of South Carolina Press, 2009.
Braxton, Joanne M., and Maria Diedrich. *Monuments of the Black Atlantic: Slavery and Memory*. Münster: LIT, 2004.
Brewer, Holly. *By Birth or Consent: Children, Law, and the Anglo-American Revolution in Authority*. Chapel Hill: University of North Carolina Press for the Omohundro Institute of Early American History and Culture, 2005.
———. "Entailing Aristocracy in Colonial Virginia and Ancient Feudal Reform: 'Ancient Feudal Restraints' and Revolutionary Reform." *William and Mary Quarterly*, 3rd ser., 54, no. 2 (1997): 307–44.
Bristol, Douglas Walter. *Knights of the Razor: Black Barbers in Slavery and Freedom*. Baltimore: Johns Hopkins University Press, 2009.
Brooks, Daphne. *Bodies in Dissent: Spectacular Performances of Race and Freedom, 1850–1910*. Durham: Duke University Press, 2006.
Brown, Kathleen M. *Foul Bodies: Cleanliness in Early America*. New Haven: Yale University Press, 2009.
———. *Good Wives, Nasty Wenches, and Anxious Patriarchs: Gender, Race, and Power in Colonial Virginia*. Chapel Hill: University of North Carolina Press for the Institute of Early American History and Culture, 1996.
Brugger, Robert. *Maryland: A Middle Temperament, 1634–1980*. Baltimore: Johns Hopkins University Press, 1996.
Burin, Eric. *The Peculiar Solution: A History of the American Colonization Society*. Gainesville: University Press of Florida, 2005.
Burke, Diane Mutti. *On Slavery's Border: Missouri's Small-Slaveholding Households, 1815–1865*. Athens: University of Georgia Press, 2010.
Bush, Barbara. "African Caribbean Slave Mothers and Children: Traumas of Dislocation and Enslavement across the Atlantic World." *Caribbean Quarterly* 56, nos. 1–2 (2010): 69–94.
———. *Slave Women in Caribbean Society, 1650–1838*. Kingston: Heinemann (Caribbean), 1990.
Bynum, Victoria. *Unruly Women: The Politics of Social and Sexual Control in the Old South*. Chapel Hill: University of North Carolina Press, 1982.
Calderhead, William L. "Anne Arundel Blacks: Three Centuries of Change." In *Anne Arundel County*, ed. Bradford, 11–25.
———. "Slavery in Maryland in the Age of Revolution, 1775–1790." *Maryland Historical Magazine* 98, no. 3 (2003): 303–24.
Calomiris, Charles W., and Jonathan B. Pritchett. "Preserving Slave Families for Profit: Traders' Incentives and Pricing in the New Orleans Slave Market." *Journal of Economic History* 69, no. 4 (2009): 986–1011.
Camp, Stephanie M. H. *Closer to Freedom: Enslaved Women and Everyday Resistance in the Plantation South*. Chapel Hill: University of North Carolina Press, 2004.

Campbell, Gwyn, Suzanne Miers, and Joseph C. Miller, eds. *Children in Slavery through the Ages*. Athens: Ohio University Press, 2009.

Campbell, Penelope. *Maryland in Africa: The Maryland State Colonization Society, 1831–1857*. Urbana: University of Illinois Press, 1971.

Carr, Lois Green. "The Development of the Maryland Orphans' Court, 1654–1715." In *Law, Society, and Politics*, ed. Land, Carr, and Papenfuse, 41–62.

Carretta, Vincent, and Ty M. Reese, eds. *The Life and Letters of Philip Quaque, the First African Anglican Missionary*. Athens: University of Georgia Press, 2010.

Clark, Emily. *The Strange History of the American Quadroon: Free Women of Color in the Revolutionary Atlantic World*. Chapel Hill: University of North Carolina Press, 2013.

Clegg, Claude. *The Price of Liberty: African Americans and the Making of Liberia*. Chapel Hill: University of North Carolina Press, 2004.

Clinton, Catherine. *The Plantation Mistress: Woman's World in the Old South*. New York: Pantheon, 1982.

Condon, Sean. "The Significance of Group Manumissions in Post-Revolutionary Rural Maryland." *Slavery and Abolition* 32, no. 1 (2011): 75–89.

———. "The Slave Owner's Family and Manumission in the Post-Revolutionary Chesapeake Tidewater: Evidence from Anne Arundel County Wills, 1790–1820." In *Paths to Freedom*, ed. Brana-Shute and Sparks, 339–62.

Cooper, Afua. *The Hanging of Angélique: The Untold Story of Canadian Slavery and the Burning of Old Montréal*. Athens: University of Georgia Press, 2007.

Cowling, Camillia. *Conceiving Freedom: Women of Color, Gender, and the Abolition of Slavery in Havana and Rio de Janeiro*. Chapel Hill: University of North Carolina Press, 2013.

———. "Debating Womanhood, Defining Freedom: The Abolition of Slavery in 1880s Rio de Janeiro." *Gender and History* 22, no. 2 (2010): 284–301.

———. "Negotiating Freedom: Women of Colour and the Transition to Free Labour in Cuba, 1870–1886." *Slavery and Abolition* 26, no. 3 (2005): 377–91.

Crais, Clifton C., and Pamela Scully. *Sara Baartman and the Hottentot Venus: A Ghost Story and a Biography*. Princeton: Princeton University Press, 2009.

Cutrafelli, Maria. *Women of Africa: Roots of Oppression*. London: Zed, 1983.

Daniels, Christine. "Alternative Workers in a Slave Economy: Kent County, Maryland, 1675–1810." PhD diss., Johns Hopkins University, 1990.

———. "'WANTED: A Blacksmith Who Understands Plantation Work': Artisans in Maryland, 1770–1810." *William and Mary Quarterly*, 3rd ser., 1, no. 4 (1993): 743–67.

Davis, Angela. "Reflections on the Black Woman's Role in the Community of Slaves." *Black Scholar* 3, no. 4 (1971): 3–14.

———. *Women, Race, and Class*. New York: Vintage, 1983.

Davis, David Brion. *Inhumane Bondage: The Rise and Fall of Slavery in the New World*. New York: Oxford University Press, 2006.

———. *The Problem of Slavery in the Age of Revolution*. 1975; New York: Oxford University Press, 1999.

Dickerson, Dennis C. *African American Preachers and Politics: The Careys of Chicago*. Jackson: University Press of Mississippi, 2010.

Donoghue, Eddie. *Black Women/White Men: The Sexual Exploitation of Female Slaves in the Danish West Indies.* Trenton, N.J.: Africa World, 2002.

Dorsey, Jennifer Hull. "Documentary History of African-American Freedom: An Introduction to the Race, Slavery and Free Blacks Microfilm Collection." *Slavery and Abolition* 30, no. 4 (2009): 545–63.

———. "Free People of Color in Rural Maryland, 1783–1832." PhD diss., Georgetown University, 2002.

———. *Hirelings: African American Workers and Free Labor in Early Maryland.* Ithaca: Cornell University Press, 2011.

Dorsey, Joseph C. "Women without History: Slavery and the International Politics of Partus Sequitur Ventrem in the Spanish Caribbean." *Journal of Caribbean History* 28, no. 2 (1994): 165–207.

Dubois, Laurent. *Avengers of the New World: The Story of the Haitian Revolution.* Cambridge: Belknap Press of Harvard University Press, 2004.

Du Bois, W. E. B. "Black Folks and Birth Control." *Birth Control Review* 16 (June 1932): 166–67.

Dunaway, Wilma A. *The African-American Family in Slavery and Emancipation.* New York: Maison des Sciences de l'Homme/Cambridge University Press, 2003.

Dunbar, Erica Armstrong. *A Fragile Freedom: African American Women and Emancipation in the Antebellum City.* New Haven: Yale University Press, 2008.

Edwards, Laura F. "Enslaved Women and the Law: Paradoxes of Subordination in the Post-Revolutionary Carolinas." *Slavery and Abolition* 26, no. 2 (2005): 305–23.

———. *Gendered Strife and Confusion: The Political Culture of Reconstruction.* Urbana: University of Illinois Press, 1997.

———. "'The Marriage Covenant Is at the Foundation of All Our Rights': The Politics of Slave Marriages in North Carolina after Emancipation." *Law and History Review* 14, no. 1 (1996): 81–124.

———. *The People and Their Peace: Legal Culture and the Transformation of Inequality in the Post-Revolutionary South.* Chapel Hill: University of North Carolina Press, 2009.

Egerton, Douglas R. *Death or Liberty: African Americans and Revolutionary America.* Oxford: Oxford University Press, 2009.

Ellison, Mary. "Resistance to Oppression: Black Women's Response to Slavery in the United States." *Slavery and Abolition* 4, no. 1 (1983): 56–63.

Eslinger, Ellen. "The Brief Career of Rufus F. Bailey, American Colonization Society Agent in Virginia." *Journal of Southern History* 71, no. 1 (2005): 39–74.

Faris, William. *The Diary of William Faris: The Daily Life of an Annapolis Silversmith.* Ed. Mark B. Letzer and Jean Burrell Russo. Baltimore: Press at the Maryland Historical Society, 2003.

Ferrer, Ada. *Freedom's Mirror: Cuba and Haiti in the Age of Revolution.* Cambridge: Cambridge University Press, 2014.

Fett, Sharla M. *Working Cures: Healing, Health, and Power on Southern Slave Plantations.* Chapel Hill: University of North Carolina Press, 2002.

Fields, Barbara Jeanne. *Slavery and Freedom on the Middle Ground: Maryland during the Nineteenth Century.* New Haven: Yale University Press, 1985.

Flannery, Eóin. "Rites of Passage: Migrancy and Liminality in Colum McCann's Songdogs and This Side of Brightness." *Irish Studies Review* 16, no. 1 (2008): 1–17.

Follett, Richard. "Heat, Sex, and Sugar: Pregnancy and Childbearing in the Slave Quarters." *Journal of Family History* 28, no. 4 (2003): 510–39.

———. "'Lives of Living Death': The Reproductive Lives of Slave Women in the Cane World of Louisiana." *Slavery and Abolition* 26, no. 2 (2005): 289–304.

Fox-Genovese, Elizabeth. *Within the Plantation Household: Black and White Women of the Old South*. Chapel Hill: University of North Carolina Press, 1988.

Franklin, John Hope. *The Free Negro in North Carolina, 1790–1860*. Chapel Hill: University of North Carolina Press, 1995.

Franklin, John Hope, and Loren Schweninger. *Runaway Slaves: Rebels on the Plantation*. New York: Oxford University Press, 1999.

Frederickson, Mary E. "A Mother's Arithmetic: Elizabeth Clark Gaines's Journey from Slavery to Freedom." In *Gendered Resistance*, ed. Frederickson and Walters, 25–48.

Frederickson, Mary E., and Delores M. Walters, eds. *Gendered Resistance: Women, Slavery, and the Legacy of Margaret Garner*. Urbana: University of Illinois Press, 2013.

Frey, Sylvia R. "Between Slavery and Freedom: Virginia Blacks in the American Revolution." *Journal of Southern History* 49, no. 3 (1983): 375–98.

———. *Water from the Rock: Black Resistance in a Revolutionary Age*. Princeton: Princeton University Press, 1991.

Frey, Sylvia R., and Betty Wood. *Come Shouting to Zion: African American Protestantism in the Americas*. Chapel Hill: University of North Carolina Press, 1998.

Fuente, Alejandro de la. "Slave Law and Claims-Making in Cuba: The Tannenbaum Debate Revisited." *Law and History Review* 22, no. 2 (2004): 339–69.

Gaspar, David Barry, and Darlene Clark Hine, eds. *Beyond Bondage: Free Women of Color in the Americas*. Urbana: University of Illinois Press, 2004.

———, eds. *More Than Chattel: Black Women and Slavery in the Americas*. Bloomington: Indiana University Press, 1996.

Gatewood, Willard B. *Aristocrats of Color: The Black Elite, 1880–1920*. Bloomington: Indiana University Press, 1990.

Genovese, Eugene. *Roll, Jordan, Roll: The World the Slaves Made*. New York: Pantheon, 1974.

Glymph, Thavolia. *Out of the House of Bondage: The Transformation of the Plantation Household*. Cambridge: Cambridge University Press, 2008.

Gomez, Michael. *Exchanging our Country Marks: The Transformation of African Identities in the Colonial and Antebellum South*. Chapel Hill: University of North Carolina Press, 1998.

Gordon-Reed, Annette. *The Hemingses of Monticello: An American Family*. New York: Norton, 2008.

Grivno, Max L. *Gleanings of Freedom: Free and Slave Labor along the Mason-Dixon Line, 1790–1860*. Urbana: University of Illinois Press, 2011.

Gutman, Herbert. *The Black Family in Slavery and Freedom, 1750–1925*. New York: Pantheon, 1976.

Ham, Deborah Newman. "The Role of African American Women in the Founding of

Liberia." In *Global Dimensions of the African Diaspora*, 2nd ed., ed. Joseph E. Harris, 369–86. Washington, D.C.: Howard University Press, 1993.

Hanger, Kimberly S. *Bounded Lives, Bounded Places: Free Black Society in Colonial New Orleans, 1769–1803*. Durham: Duke University Press, 1997.

Hansen, Austin. *Reaching Out: An Epic of the People of St. Philip's Church*. New York: St. Philip's Church, 1986.

Harris, Cheryl I. "Whiteness as Property." *Harvard Law Review* 106, no. 8 (1993): 1707–91.

Harris, Leslie M. *In the Shadow of Slavery: African Americans in New York City, 1626–1863*. Chicago: University of Chicago Press, 2003.

Hartman, Saidiya V. *Lose Your Mother: A Journey along the Atlantic Slave Route*. New York: Farrar, Straus, and Giroux, 2007.

———. *Scenes of Subjection: Terror, Slavery, and Self-Making in Nineteenth-Century America*. New York: Oxford University Press, 1997.

Hayre, Ruth Wright, and Alexis Moore. *Tell Them We Are Rising: A Memoir of Faith in Education*. New York: Wiley, 1997.

Herndon, Ruth Wallis. *Unwelcome Americans: Living on the Margin in Early New England*. Philadelphia: University of Pennsylvania Press, 2001.

Heuman, Gad J., and Trevor G. Burnard, eds. *The Routledge History of Slavery*. London: Routledge, 2011.

Heuman, Gad J., and James Walvin, eds. *The Slavery Reader*. London: Routledge, 2003.

Hine, Darlene Clark. *Hine Sight: Black Women and the Re-Construction of American History*. Brooklyn, N.Y.: Carlson, 1994.

Hine, Darlene Clark, and Kate Wittenstein. "Female Slave Resistance: The Economics of Sex." In *Black Woman Cross-Culturally*, ed. Steady, 289–99.

Hobson, Janell. *Body as Evidence: Mediating Race, Globalizing Gender*. Albany: State University of New York Press, 2012.

Hodes, Martha. "Sally Hemings, Founding Mother." *Reviews in American History* 38, no. 3 (2010): 437–42.

———, ed. *Sex, Love, Race: Crossing Boundaries in North American History*. New York: New York University Press, 1999.

———. *White Women, Black Men: Illicit Sex in the Nineteenth-Century South*. New Haven: Yale University Press, 1997.

Hoffman, Ronald, and Peter J. Albert, eds. *Women in the Age of the American Revolution*. Charlottesville: University Press of Virginia for the U.S. Capitol Historical Society, 1989.

Horton, James Oliver, and Lois E. Horton. *In Hope of Liberty: Culture, Community, and Protest among Northern Free Blacks, 1700–1860*. New York: Oxford University Press, 1997.

Hudson, Larry. *To Have and to Hold: Slave Work and Family Life in Antebellum South Carolina*. Athens: University of Georgia Press, 1997.

Humez, Jean McMahon. *Harriet Tubman: The Life and the Life Stories*. Madison: University of Wisconsin Press, 2003.

Hunter, Tera W. *To 'Joy My Freedom: Southern Black Women's Lives and Labors after the Civil War*. Cambridge: Harvard University Press, 1997.

Isaacs, Rhys. *The Transformation of Virginia, 1740–1790*. New York: Norton, 1982.
James, Winston. *The Struggles of John Brown Russwurm: The Life and Writings of a Pan-Africanist Pioneer, 1799–1851*. New York: New York University Press, 2010.
Jensen, Niklas Thode. *For the Health of the Enslaved: Slaves, Medicine, and Power in the Danish West Indies, 1803–1848*. Copenhagen: Museum Tusculanum, 2012.
John, Marie-Elena. *Unburnable*. New York: Amistad, 2006.
Johnson, Michael P., and James L. Roark. *Black Masters: A Free Family of Color in the Old South*. New York: Norton, 1984.
Johnson, Walter, ed. *The Chattel Principle: Internal Slave Trades in the Americas*. New Haven: Yale University Press, 2004.
———. "On Agency." *Journal of Social History* 37, no. 1 (2003): 113–23.
———. *River of Dark Dreams: Slavery and Empire in the Cotton Kingdom*. Cambridge: Belknap Press of Harvard University Press, 2013.
———. *Soul by Soul: Life inside the Antebellum Slave Market*. Cambridge: Harvard University Press, 1999.
Jones, Anne Goodwyn, and Susan V. Donaldson, eds. *Haunted Bodies: Gender and Southern Texts*. Charlottesville: University Press of Virginia, 1997.
Jones, Jacqueline. "The Mixed Legacy of the American Revolution for Black Women." In *Major Problems in American Women's History: Documents and Essays*, 3rd ed., ed. Mary Beth Norton and Ruth M. Alexander, 96–100. Boston: Houghton Mifflin, 2003.
———. "Race, Sex, and Self-Evident Truths: The Status of Slave Women during the Era of the American Revolution." In *Women in the Age of the American Revolution*, ed. Hoffman and Albert, 293–337.
Jones, Martha S. "The Case of Jean Baptiste, un Créole de Saint-Domingue: Narrating Slavery, Freedom, and the Haitian Revolution in Baltimore City." In *The American South and the Atlantic World*, ed. B. Ward, M. Bone, and W. A. Link, 104–28. Gainesville: University Press of Florida, 2013.
Kamoie, Laura Croghan. *Irons in the Fire: The Business History of the Tayloe Family and Virginia's Gentry, 1700–1860*. Charlottesville: University of Virginia Press, 2007.
Kaye, Anthony E. *Joining Places: Slave Neighborhoods in the Old South*. Chapel Hill: University of North Carolina Press, 2007.
King, Wilma. *The Essence of Liberty: Free Black Women during the Slave Era*. Columbia: University of Missouri Press, 2006.
———. "Out of Bounds: Emancipated and Enslaved Women in Antebellum America." In *Beyond Bondage*, ed. Gaspar and Hine, 127–45.
———. *Stolen Childhood: Slave Youth in Nineteenth-Century America*. Bloomington: Indiana University Press, 1995.
Koger, Larry. *Black Slaveowners: Free Black Slave Masters in South Carolina, 1790–1860*. Jefferson, N.C.: McFarland, 1985.
Konadu, Kwasi. *The Akan Diaspora in the Americas*. Oxford: Oxford University Press, 2010.
Krauthamer, Barbara. "Ar'n't I a Woman?: Native Americans, Gender, and Slavery." *Journal of Women's History* 19, no. 2 (2007): 156–60.
Kulikoff, Allan. *Tobacco and Slaves: The Development of Southern Cultures in the Chesapeake, 1680–1800*. Chapel Hill: University of North Carolina Press, 1986.

Lancaster, Kent. "Chattel Slavery at Hampton/Northampton, Baltimore County." *Maryland Historical Magazine* 95, no. 4 (2000): 409–28.

Land, Aubrey C., Lois Green Carr, and Edward C. Papenfuse, eds. *Law, Society, and Politics in Early Maryland: Proceedings of the First Conference on Maryland History, June 14–15, 1974*. Baltimore: Johns Hopkins University Press, 1977.

Lebsock, Suzanne. *The Free Women of Petersburg: Status and Culture in a Southern Town, 1784–1860*. New York: Norton, 1985.

Lee, Channa Kai. *For Freedom's Sake: The Life of Fannie Lou Hamer*. Urbana: University of Illinois Press, 2000.

Leone, Mark P. *The Archaeology of Liberty in an American Capital: Excavations in Annapolis*. Berkeley: University of California Press, 2005.

Leslie, Kent Anderson. *Woman of Color, Daughter of Privilege: Amanda America Dickson, 1849–1893*. Athens: University of Georgia Press, 1995.

Levine, Lawrence W. *Black Culture and Black Consciousness: Afro-American Folk Thought from Slavery to Freedom*. New York: Oxford University Press, 1977.

Link, William A., ed. *Creating Citizenship in the Nineteenth-Century South*. Gainesville: University Press of Florida, 2013.

Litwack, Leon. *Been in the Storm So Long: The Aftermath of Slavery*. New York: Vintage, 1979.

Lum, Kenneth Anthony. *Praising His Name in the Dance: Spirit Possession in the Spiritual Baptist Faith and Orisha Work in Trinidad, West Indies*. Australia: Harwood Academic, 2000.

Mair, Lucille Mathurin, and Dennis Ranston. *The Rebel Woman in the British West Indies during Slavery*. Kingston: Institute of Jamaica Publications, 1995.

McDaniel, Cecily Barker, and Tekla Ali Johnson, eds. *Africana Legacy: Diasporic Studies in the Americas*. Littleton, Mass.: Tapestry, 2007.

McDonald, Robert M. S. "Race, Sex, and Reputation: Thomas Jefferson and the Sally Hemings Story." *Southern Cultures* 4, no. 2 (1998): 46–63.

McLaurin, Melton Alonza. *Celia, a Slave*. Athens: University of Georgia Press, 1991.

Miles, Tiya. *The House on Diamond Hill: A Cherokee Plantation Story*. Chapel Hill: University of North Carolina Press, 2010.

———. *Ties That Bind: The Story of an Afro-Cherokee Family in Slavery and Freedom*. Berkeley: University of California Press, 2005.

Miles, Tiya, and Sharon Patricia Holland. *Crossing Waters, Crossing Worlds: The African Diaspora in Indian Country*. Durham: Duke University Press, 2006.

Millward, Jessica. "Charity Folks, Lost Royalty, and the Bishop Family of Maryland and New York." *Journal of African American History* 98, no. 1 (2013): 24–47.

———. "More History Than Myth: African American Women's History since the Publication of *Ar'n't I a Woman?*" *Journal of Women's History* 19, no. 2 (2007): 161–67.

———. "'The Relics of Slavery': Interracial Sex and Manumission in the American South." *Frontiers: A Journal of Women's Studies* 31, no. 3 (2010): 22–30.

———. "'That All Her Increase Shall Be Free': Enslaved Women's Bodies and the Maryland 1809 Law of Manumission." *Women's History Review* 21, no. 3 (2012): 363–78.

Mitchell, Michele. *Righteous Propagation: African Americans and the Politics of Racial Destiny after Reconstruction*. Chapel Hill: University of North Carolina Press, 2004.

Morgan, Jennifer L. "Gender and Family Life." In *Routledge History of Slavery*, ed. Heuman and Bernard, 157–74.

———. *Laboring Women: Reproduction and Gender in New World Slavery*. Philadelphia: University of Pennsylvania Press, 2004.

———. "'Some Could Suckle over Their Shoulder': Male Travelers, Female Bodies, and the Gendering of Racial Ideology, 1500–1770." *William and Mary Quarterly*, 3rd ser., 54, no. 1 (1997): 167–92.

Morgan, Kenneth. "Slave Women and Reproduction in Jamaica, c. 1776–1834." *History* 91, no. 302 (2006): 231–53.

Morgan, Philip D. *Slave Counterpoint: Black Culture in the Eighteenth-Century Chesapeake and Lowcountry*. Chapel Hill: University of North Carolina Press for the Omohundro Institute of Early American History and Culture, 1998.

Morrison, Toni. *Beloved: A Novel*. New York: Random House, 1987.

———. *Playing in the Dark: Whiteness and the Literary Imagination*. Cambridge: Harvard University Press, 1992.

Moynihan, Daniel. *The Negro Family: The Case for National Action*. Washington, D.C.: U.S. Department of Labor, 1965.

Mullin, Gerald. *Flight and Rebellion: Slave Resistance in Eighteenth-Century Virginia*. Oxford: Oxford University Press, 1972.

Mullins, Paul R. *Race and Affluence: An Archaeology of African America and Consumer Culture*. New York: Kluwer Academic/Plenum, 1999.

Mustakeem, Sowande'. "'Make Haste and Let Me See You with a Good Cargo of Negroes': Gender, Health, and Violence in the Eighteenth Century Middle Passage." In *Gender, Race, Ethnicity, and Power in Maritime America*, ed. Glenn Gordinier, 3–21. Mystic, Conn.: Mystic Seaport Museum, 2008.

———. "'She Must Go Overboard & Shall Go Overboard': Diseased Bodies and the Spectacle of Murder at Sea." *Atlantic Studies* 8, no. 3 (2011): 301–16.

Myers, Amrita Chakrabarti. *Forging Freedom: Black Women and the Pursuit of Liberty in Antebellum Charleston*. Chapel Hill: University of North Carolina Press, 2011.

Nash, Gary B. *Forging Freedom: The Formation of Philadelphia's Black Community, 1720–1840*. Cambridge: Harvard University Press, 1988.

Nathans, Sydney. *To Free a Family: The Journey of Mary Walker*. Cambridge: Harvard University Press, 2012.

Nicolaisen, Peter. "Thomas Jefferson, Sally Hemings, and the Question of Race: An Ongoing Debate." *Journal of American Studies* 37, no. 1 (2003): 99–118.

Norton, Mary Beth. "The Fate of Some Black Loyalists of the American Revolution." *Journal of Negro History* 58, no. 4 (1973): 402–26.

Norton, Mary Beth, Herbert G. Gutman, and Ira Berlin. "The Afro-American Family in the Age of Revolution." In *Slavery and Freedom in the Age of the American Revolution*, ed. Ira Berlin and Ronald Hoffman, 173–91. Charlottesville: University of Virginia Press, 1983.

O'Malley, Gregory. "Final Passages: The British Inter-Colonial Slave Trade, 1619–1807." PhD diss., Johns Hopkins University, 2006.

Painter, Nell Irvin. *Sojourner Truth: A Life, a Symbol*. New York: Norton, 1996.

———. *Soul Murder and Slavery*. Waco, Tex.: Markham Fund, Baylor University Press, 1995.

———. "Soul Murder and Slavery: Toward a Fully Loaded Cost Accounting." In *U.S. History as Women's History*, ed. Linda K. Kerber, 125–46. Chapel Hill: University of North Carolina Press, 1995.

Papenfuse, Eric Robert. "From Redcompense to Revolution: Mahoney v. Ashton and the Transfiguration of Maryland Culture, 1791–1802." *Slavery and Abolition* 15, no. 3 (1994): 38–62.

Pargas, Damian Alan. "Disposing of Human Property: American Slave Families and Forced Separation in Comparative Perspective." *Journal of Family History* 34, no. 3 (2009): 251–74.

———. *The Quarters and the Fields: Slave Families in the Non-Cotton South*. Gainesville: University Press of Florida, 2010.

Pascoe, Peggy. *What Comes Naturally: Miscegenation Law and the Making of Race in America*. Oxford: Oxford University Press, 2009.

Patterson, Orlando. *Slavery and Social Death: A Comparative Study*. Cambridge: Harvard University Press, 1982.

Penningroth, Dylan C. *The Claims of Kinfolk: African American Property and Community in the Nineteenth-Century South*. Chapel Hill: University of North Carolina Press, 2003.

Perbi, Akosua Adoma. *A History of Indigenous Slavery in Ghana: From the 15th to the 19th Century*. Legon, Accra, Ghana: Sub-Saharan, 2005.

Perrin, Liese M. "Resisting Reproduction: Reconsidering Slave Contraception in the Old South." *Journal of American Studies* 35, no. 2 (2001): 255–74.

Phillips, Christopher. *Freedom's Port: The African American Community of Baltimore, 1790–1860*. Urbana: University of Illinois Press, 1997.

Pybus, Cassandra. *Epic Journeys of Freedom: Runaway Slaves of the American Revolution and Their Global Quest for Liberty*. Boston: Beacon, 2006.

Quarles, Benjamin. *The Negro in the American Revolution*. Chapel Hill: University of North Carolina Press for the Institute of Early American History and Culture, 1961.

Rabin, Dana. "'In a Country of Liberty?': Slavery, Villeinage, and the Making of Whiteness in the Somerset Case (1772)." *History Workshop Journal* 72, no. 1 (2011): 5–29.

Raboteau, Albert J. *Slave Religion: The "Invisible Institution" in the Antebellum South*. New York: Oxford University Press, 1978.

Ransby, Barbara. *Ella Baker and the Black Freedom Movement: A Radical Democratic Vision*. Chapel Hill: University of North Carolina Press, 2003.

Reddock, Rhoda E. "Women and Slavery in the Caribbean: A Feminist Perspective." *Latin American Perspectives*, 12, no. 1 (Winter 1985): 63–80.

Reese, Ty M. "Facilitating the Slave Trade: Company Slaves at Cape Coast Castle, 1750–1807." *Slavery and Abolition* 31, no. 3 (2010): 363–77.

Reid, Patricia A. "Margaret Morgan's Story: A Threshold between Slavery and Freedom, 1820–1842." *Slavery and Abolition* 33, no. 3 (2012): 359–80.

Reinhardt, Mark. "Who Speaks for Margaret Garner?: Slavery, Silence, and the Politics of Ventriloquism." *Critical Inquiry* 29, no. 1 (2002): 81–119.

———. *Who Speaks for Margaret Garner?* Minneapolis: University of Minnesota Press, 2010.

Roberts, Dorothy E. *Killing the Black Body: Race, Reproduction, and the Meaning of Liberty*. New York: Pantheon, 1997.

———. "Welfare and the Problem of Black Citizenship." *Yale Law Journal* 105, no. 6 (1996): 1563–1602.
Rockman, Seth. *Scraping By: Wage Labor, Slavery, and Survival in Early Baltimore.* Baltimore: Johns Hopkins University Press, 2009.
———. "Women's Labor, Gender Ideology, and Working Class Households in Early Republic Baltimore." *Pennsylvania History* 66 (1999): 174–200.
Rothman, Joshua D. *Notorious in the Neighborhood: Sex and Families across the Color Line in Virginia, 1787–1861.* Chapel Hill: University of North Carolina Press, 2003.
Rucker, Walter C. *The River Flows On: Black Resistance, Culture, and Identity Formation in Early America.* Baton Rouge: Louisiana State University Press, 2006.
Russo, Jean B. "Chesapeake Artisans in the Aftermath of the American Revolution." In *The Transforming Hand of the Revolution: Reconsidering the American Revolution as a Social Movement*, ed. Ronald Hoffman and Peter J. Albert, 118–54. Charlottesville: University Press of Virginia for the U.S. Capitol Historical Society, 1996.
Saillant, John. "The Black Body Erotic and the Republican Body Politic, 1790–1820." *Journal of the History of Sexuality* 5, no. 3 (1995): 403–28.
Saville, Julie. *The Work of Reconstruction: From Slave to Wage Laborer in South Carolina, 1860–1870.* Cambridge: Cambridge University Press, 1994.
Schermerhorn, Calvin. *Money over Mastery, Family over Freedom: Slavery in the Antebellum Upper South.* Baltimore: Johns Hopkins University Press, 2011.
Schwalm, Leslie A. *A Hard Fight for We: Women's Transition from Slavery to Freedom in South Carolina.* Urbana: University of Illinois Press, 1997.
Schwartz, Marie Jenkins. *Birthing a Slave: Motherhood and Medicine in the Antebellum South.* Cambridge: Harvard University Press, 2006.
Schweninger, Loren. *Black Property Owners in the South, 1790–1915.* Urbana: University of Illinois Press, 1990.
———. "The Fragile Nature of Freedom: Free Women of Color in the U.S. South." In *Beyond Bondage*, ed. Gaspar and Hine, 106–27.
———. "Freedom Suits, African American Women, and the Genealogy of Slavery." *William and Mary Quarterly* 71, no. 1 (2014): 35–62.
———. "Property Owning Free African-American Women in the South, 1800–1870." *Journal of Women's History* 1, no. 3 (1990): 13–44.
Scott, Rebecca J. *Degrees of Freedom: Louisiana and Cuba after Slavery.* Cambridge: Belknap Press of Harvard University Press, 2005.
Scully, Pamela, and Diana Paton, eds. *Gender and Slave Emancipation in the Atlantic World.* Durham: Duke University Press, 2005.
Shackel, Paul A., and Barbara J. Little, eds. *Historical Archaeology of the Chesapeake.* Washington, D.C.: Smithsonian Institution Press, 1994.
Sharpe, Jenny. *Ghosts of Slavery: A Literary Archaeology of Black Women's Lives.* Minneapolis: University of Minnesota Press, 2003.
Shepherd, Verene, ed. *Working Slavery, Pricing Freedom: Perspectives from the Caribbean, Africa, and the African Diaspora.* New York: Palgrave, 2002.
Shohat, Ella, ed. *Talking Visions: Multicultural Feminism in a Transnational Age.* New York: New Museum of Contemporary Art; Cambridge: MIT Press, 1998.
Sidbury, James. *Becoming African in America: Race and Nation in the Early Black Atlantic.* Oxford: Oxford University Press, 2007.

Smith, Merril D., ed. *Sex without Consent: Rape and Sexual Coercion in America*. New York: New York University Press, 2001.

Smithers, Gregory D. "American Abolitionism and Slave-Breeding Discourse: A Re-Evaluation." *Slavery and Abolition* 33, no. 4 (2012): 551–70.

———. *Slave Breeding: Sex, Violence, and Memory in African American History*. Gainesville: University Press of Florida, 2012.

Spear, Jennifer M. *Race, Sex, and Social Order in Early New Orleans*. Baltimore: Johns Hopkins University Press, 2009.

Spruill, Julia Cherry. *Women's Life and Work in the Southern Colonies*. New York: Norton, 1972.

Stanley, Amy Dru. *From Bondage to Contract: Wage Labor, Marriage, and the Market in the Age of Slave Emancipation*. Cambridge: Cambridge University Press, 1998.

Steady, Filomina Chioma, ed. *The Black Woman Cross-Culturally*. Cambridge, Mass.: Schenkman, 1981.

———, ed. *Black Women, Globalization, and Economic Justice: Studies from Africa and the African Diaspora*. Rochester, Vt.: Schenkman, 2001.

Stevenson, Brenda. "Black Family Structure." In *Decline in Marriage*, ed. Tucker and Mitchell-Kernan, 27–56.

———. "Distress and Discord in Virginia Slave Families, 1830–1860." In *In Joy and in Sorrow*, ed. Bleser, 103–25.

———. "Gender Convention, Ideals, and Identity among Antebellum Virginia Slave Women." In *More Than Chattel*, ed. Gaspar and Hine, 169–90.

———. *Life in Black and White: Family and Community in the Slave South*. New York: Oxford University Press, 1996.

Stuckey, Sterling. *Slave Culture: Nationalist Theory and the Foundations of Black America*. New York: Oxford University Press, 1987.

Sweet, James H. *Recreating Africa: Culture, Kinship, and Religion in the African-Portuguese World, 1441–1770*. Chapel Hill: University of North Carolina Press, 2003.

Tadman, Michael. "The Demographic Cost of Sugar: Debates on Slave Societies and Natural Increase in the Americas." *American Historical Review* 105, no. 5 (2000): 1534–75.

———. *Speculators and Slaves: Masters, Traders, and Slaves in the Old South*. Madison: University of Wisconsin Press, 1989.

Taylor, Alan. *The Internal Enemy: Slavery and War in Virginia, 1772–1832*. New York: Norton, 2013.

Taylor, Ula. "Feminism." In *Black Women in America*, 2nd ed., ed. Darlene Clark Hine, 435–43. New York: Oxford University Press, 2005.

———. *The Veiled Garvey: The Life and Times of Amy Jacques Garvey*. Chapel Hill: University of North Carolina Press, 2002.

Thompson, Shirley Elizabeth. *Exiles at Home: The Struggle to Become American in Creole New Orleans*. Cambridge: Harvard University Press, 2009.

Tucker, M. Belinda, and Claudia Mitchell-Kernan, eds. *The Decline in Marriage among African Americans: Causes, Consequences, and Policy Implications*. Thousand Oaks, Calif.: Sage, 1995.

Turner, Sasha. "Home-Grown Slaves: Women, Reproduction, and the Abolition of the Slave Trade, Jamaica 1788–1807." *Journal of Women's History* 23, no. 3 (2011): 39–62.

Tyler-McGraw, Marie. *An African Republic: Black and White Virginians in the Making of Liberia*. Chapel Hill: University of North Carolina Press, 2007.

Wallace, Barbara. "'Fair Daughters of Africa': African American Women in Baltimore, 1790–1860." PhD diss., University of California, Los Angeles, 2001.

Walsh, Lorena S. "Feeding the Eighteenth-Century Town Folk; or, Whence the Beef?" *Agricultural History* 73, no. 3 (1999): 267–80.

———. *Provisioning Early American Towns: The Chesapeake: A Multidisciplinary Case Study*. Final Performance Report, National Endowment for the Humanities Grant RO-22643-93. Williamsburg, Va.: Colonial Williamsburg Foundation, 1977.

———. "Urban Amenities and Rural Sufficiency: Living Standards and Consumer Behavior in the Colonial Chesapeake, 1643–1777." *Journal of Economic History* 43, no. 1 (1983): 109–17.

Walters, Delores M. "Introduction: Re(dis)covering and Recreating the Cultural Milieu of Margaret Garner." In *Gendered Resistance*, ed. Frederickson and Walters, 25–48.

Warren, Wendy A. "More Than Words: Language, Colonization, and History." *William and Mary Quarterly* 69, no. 3 (2012): 517–20.

———. "The Cause of Her Grief: The Rape of a Slave in Early New England." *Journal of American History* 93, no. 4 (2007): 1031–49.

Washington, Margaret. *Sojourner Truth's America*. Urbana: University of Illinois Press, 2009.

Weinbaum, Alys Eve. "Gendering the General Strike: W. E. B. Du Bois's *Black Reconstruction* and Black Feminism's 'Propaganda of History.'" *South Atlantic Quarterly* 112, no. 3 (2013): 437–63.

Wesley, Marilyn C. "A Woman's Place: The Politics of Space in Harriet Jacobs's *Incidents in the Life of a Slave Girl*." *Women's Studies* 26, no. 1 (1997): 59–72.

West, Emily. *Chains of Love: Slave Couples in Antebellum South Carolina*. Urbana: University of Illinois Press, 2004.

———. "The Debate on the Strength of Slave Families: South Carolina and the Importance of Cross-Plantation Marriages." *Journal of American Studies* 33, no. 2 (1999): 221–41.

White, Deborah Gray. *Ar'n't I a Woman?: Female Slaves in the Plantation South*. New York: Norton, 1985.

Whitman, T. Stephen. *Challenging Slavery in the Chesapeake: Black and White Resistance to Human Bondage, 1775–1865*. Baltimore: Maryland Historical Society, 2007.

———. "Manumission and Apprenticeship in Maryland, 1770–1870." *Maryland Historical Magazine* 101, no. 1 (2006): 55–71.

———. *The Price of Freedom: Slavery and Manumission in Baltimore and Early National Maryland*. Lexington: University Press of Kentucky, 1997.

Wilder, L. Douglas. "The U.S. National Slavery Museum." *Virginia Tomorrow*, March 11, 2009. http://virginiatomorrow.com/2009/03/11/the-us-national-slavery-museum/.

Williams, Eric Eustace. *Capitalism and Slavery*. New York: Russell and Russell, 1961.

Williams, Heather Andrea. *Help Me to Find My People: The African American Search for Family Lost in Slavery*. Chapel Hill: University of North Carolina Press, 2012.

Winch, Julie. *The Clamorgans: One Family's History of Race in America*. New York: Hill and Wang, 2011.

Windham, Joseph E. "Bondage, Bias, and the Bench: An Historical Analysis of Maryland Court of Appeals Cases Involving Blacks, 1830–1860." PhD diss., Howard University, 1990.

Woodson, Carter G. *Free Negro Owners of Slaves in the United States in 1830, Together with Absentee Owners of Slaves in the United States in 1830*. 1924; New York: Negro Universities Press, 1968.

Young, Hershini Bhana. *Haunting Capital: Memory, Text, and the Black Diasporic Body*. Hanover, N.H.: University Press of New England, 2006.

Young, Jason R. *Rituals of Resistance: African Atlantic Religion in Kongo and the Lowcountry South in the Era of Slavery*. Baton Rouge: Louisiana State University Press, 2007.

Zipf, Karen. "Reconstructing 'Free Woman': African-American Women, Apprenticeship, and Custody Rights during Reconstruction." *Journal of Women's History* 12, no. 1 (2000): 8–31.

INDEX

Note: Place names refer to Maryland unless otherwise qualified.

abolitionists, xx, 17, 59
abortion, 19, 80n36
Act Related to Freeing Slaves by Will or Testament of 1790 (Md.), 10–11
Act to Ascertain and Declare the Condition of Such Issue as May Hereafter Be Born of Negro or Mulatto Female Slaves of 1809 (Md.), 12, 35, 36; three significant implications of, 37
Adams, Catherine, 3, 28
Adams, John (free black), 48
African Americans: citizenship and, 2, 58; class standing and, 63; historical awareness of, 68–69; importance of family to, 51; meaning of manhood to, 58; network types, 85n58; in post–Civil War, 41, 43; prominent churches of, 70; prominent families of, xviii; U.S. advancement of, 59; violence against, 70. *See also* enslaved women; free blacks; slavery
African colonization movement, 39, 57, 58–59
African Methodist Episcopal Church, 59, 68
African society, xix, 41–44, 46, 51, 52; herbal lore and, 8–9, 43; matrifocal kinship and, 57; Middle Passage and, 16–17, 41, 43; spiritual practices and, 8, 11, 43
"afterlife of slavery" concept, 12
agency, 6, 7, 14, 29, 40, 54, 55, 57
Age of Revolution (1763–1823), 2–6, 29–40; definition of, 77n25
agricultural work. *See* farming
Akan people, 41, 42, 43–44, 46
Alexander, Leslie, 3–4
Allen, Richard, 59
almshouses, 65, 66

American Colonization Society, 57, 58, 59
American Revolution, xix, xx, 4, 10, 12, 43, 77n25; black participants in, 3; equality/liberty language of, 31, 50; freedom petitions following, 29–31, 39
Angelique (enslaved woman), 3
Anna Maria (enslaved woman), 18
Annapolis, xvii, xix, 29, 31, 50; archeological site, xviii, 11, 68; Banneker-Douglass Museum, 68, 73; Bishop family and, 51, 68, 69–70; Charity's life in, 5, 8, 22, 26, 55, 60, 68, 73; Folks and Bishop families' gravesites in, 67–68, 70–71, 73–74; free black residents of, xviii, 55, 56, 61, 65; Haley memorial, xx, 68–69, 73; Historic Annapolis Foundation, xviii, 69; Reconciliation March (2004), 68; Ridout family and, xix, 8, 11, 22, 26, 52, 55, 68, 73; slaveholding society of, 8, 23–24, 81n62; slavery's legacies in, 68–69; as state capital, 5
Anne Arundel County, 5, 9, 21, 48, 50, 57; African American wealth and, 61; apprenticeships and, 63, 64, 65, 66; enslaved blacks (1790), 5; free black household sites, 55; manumission records, xviii, 23–24, 37–38, 46, 47, 51. *See also* Annapolis
Anne Arundel County Court, 52, 63
Anne Arundel Orphan's Court, 64
antislavery groups, 4, 30; abolitionists, xx, 17, 59
apprenticeships, 13, 50, 53, 54, 55, 63–66
Arawaks, 28
Archeology in Annapolis project, xviii, 11, 68
Ar'n't I a Woman? (White), 3
Arsene (enslaved woman), 10
artisans, 64
Ashburn, Mary, 9

119

INDEX

Ashton, John, 32, 33
Atlantic slave trade. *See* international slave trade
autonomy, 6, 8, 12

Baartman, Sara, xvii
Badger, Benjamin, 48
Bailey, Harriet, 20
bakers, 61
Baltimore City, xx, 8, 19, 23, 44, 56–57; almshouse racial composition, 65; apprenticeships, 63, 64, 65; black female-male ratio, 56; black women's freedom potential, 29; domestic slave trade, 52; free black residents of, xviii, 4, 36, 55–56, 63, 65; port of, 5; St. Mary's Parish Church, 70; slaveholding society of, 9–10, 23–24
Baltimore County, 5, 9, 18, 48, 55, 66; freedom petitions, 34; manumission documents, xviii
Baltimore County Ironworks, 9, 81n62
Bank of America building (Annapolis), 68, 73
Banneker-Douglass Museum (Annapolis), 68, 73
Baptiste, Jean, 30
barbers, 61, 65
Barrow, George, 64
Beale, Thomas, 31
beige aristocracy, 63
Belair Plantation, xvii, 22, 68
Bentan, Albert, 64
Berlin, Ira, 8, 30, 63, 69
Berry, George, 50
biblical language, 74
birth control, 19, 20, 80n36
Bishop, Charity Folks (Lil' Charity; Charity's daughter), xviii–xix, xx, 60–61, 63, 67–68, 73–74; childhood of, 26, 59; headstone of, 70–71; manumission and, 42, 51, 52; as mother's favorite, 56, 59; six children of, 56, 70; wealth of, 62, 69–70
Bishop, Elizabeth Chew (William Henry's wife), 70
Bishop, Eloise Carey (Shelton Hale's wife), 70
Bishop, Horace (Charity's grandson), 58
Bishop, Horace (William II's brother), 47
Bishop, Dr. Hutchens Chew (Charity's great-grandson), 70
Bishop, James Calder (Charity's grandson), 70

Bishop, John T. (Charity's great-grandson), 74
Bishop, Moses Lake (Charity's grandson), 65, 70, 74
Bishop, Nicholas (Charity's grandson), 58, 62
Bishop, Rebecca (Peter Vogelsang's wife; Charity's granddaughter), 70, 74
Bishop, Rebecca (William II's sister), 47
Bishop, Rev. Shelton Hale (Charity's great-great grandson), 70, 73
Bishop, William, Sr. ("Daddy Bishop"), 24–25, 47
Bishop, William, II (Charity's son-in-law), xviii, 24, 63; children of, 56, 70; family burial plot of, 67–68, 70–71, 73–74; manumission of, 47; property owned by, 68, 69–70; wealth of, 61, 62, 65, 69–70
Bishop, William Henry, III (Charity's grandson), 62, 65, 70
Bishop, Dr. William, IV (Charity's great-grandson), 74
"blackness." *See* skin color
blacksmiths, 61, 65
Blake, Margaret Jane, 51
Block, Sharon, 18
Bond, Thomas, 18
bondspeople. *See* slavery
bondswomen. *See* enslaved women
Booth, Catherine, 34
Booth, Esther, 34
Booth, Richard, 34
Booth, Sally, 34
Boothe, Edward, 61
Boston family, 27, 28, 32
Boswell, Walter, 58
Bowie Museums, 68
Brackett, Jeffrey, 61
Brandt, Randolph Latimer, 58
Brice, Hercules, 61
bricklayers, 61
Britain, anti-slavery measures, 14, 17, 32, 77n25
Brown, Vachel and Paul, 49
Brown family, 32
builders, 61
Burke, Elizabeth Machubin, 38
Burke, James (Charity's brother), 22, 25, 42
Burke, John M., 38
Burke, Rachel (Charity's mother), 21–23, 25–26, 42, 54
Bush, Barbara, 19

Butler, Absalom, 64
Butler, Charles ("Negro Charles"), 31
Butler, Eleanor, 31–32
Butler, Mary, 31, 32
Butler, William, 31–32

Calder, Ann (Charity's granddaughter), 53
Calder, Harriet Jackson (Charity's daughter), 26, 42, 52, 53, 56, 57; guardianship of enslaved children of, 53, 62
Calder, James (Charity's grandson), 53
Calder, William (Charity's son-in-law), 53, 56
Calder, William, Jr. (Charity's grandson), 53
Calderhead, William, 61
Caldwell, Isabell, 29
Callahan, Mary, 47
Campbell, Glenn, xviii, xix
Capitol, U.S., Douglass statue at, xx
Carey, Eloise (Shelton Hale Bishop's wife), 70
Caribbean area, 16, 19, 28
Carroll, Charles, 11, 21, 33
Carroll family, 9, 45, 81n62
Carrollton, 21, 33, 45
Carter family, 9, 81n62
Catholic Church, 11, 33, 73
"Celia, a slave," xvii
Census, U.S. (1790), 5, 26
Census, U.S. (1800), 50
Census, U.S. (1810), 5, 26
Census, U.S. (1820), 5, 26, 62
charity (biblical term), 74
"Charity Folks, Lost Royalty, and the Bishop Family of Maryland and New York" (Millward), xx
Charles County, 20
Charleston, S.C., 10
Chesapeake, 61, 86n62; manumission laws, 16; waterways, 8
Chesapeake Bay, 5
childbearing. *See* mothers; reproduction
children: apprenticeship of, 13, 50, 53, 54, 55, 63–65; entail and, 18, 48; fathers and, 16, 20, 37, 54, 57; freedom petitions and, 12, 27, 35, 39; freedom purchased for, 47–48, 50; gradual emancipation of, 48; grandparent guardians, 58; hiring out of, 44; inherited slave status of, 12, 14, 15–16, 18–19, 21, 24–25, 31, 35–37, 51; manumission conditions for, 10, 12, 15, 24–25, 36, 46–47, 48; orphans' courts, 11, 50, 63, 64, 65, 66; resistance strategies taught to, 15; separation from mothers, 44–45
Christian belief, 11. *See also* religion; *and specific churches*
Church Circle (Annapolis), 60, 68
Cincinnati, Underground Railroad Freedom Center, 69
citizenship, 2, 58
City of Bowie Museums, 68
city slaves, advantages of, 9–10
Civil War, xviii, xx, 43; Reconstruction period, 52, 66
Clark, Emily, 23
class division, 60, 61, 63, 69
coal, 9
coartación, 46
colonization movement, African, 39, 57, 58–59
color consciousness. *See* skin color
Columbia University, 70
community, 3–4, 10, 41–52; networks of, 7, 41, 43, 47; women's forming of, 19, 20
Conaway, Cornelius, 17
Condon, Sean, 46, 51
Constitution, U.S., international slave trade ban, 35
Constitution, USS, 70
Cook, Mary, 18
Cooper, Afua, 3
Corinthians, First Epistle to the, 1, 14, 27, 41, 53, 67, 74
Cornhill Street (Annapolis), 56
Cornish, William, 44
cosmogram, 11
Court of Appeals for the Western Shore, 38
Cowling, Camillia, 2, 14, 29
Creek, Margaret, 34
crops. *See* farming
Cuba, 2, 14, 29
Cullen, Countee, 70
curfews, 63, 66
Cutrafelli, Maria, 19

Davidson, John, 42, 45, 55, 68
Davidson, Thomas, 50
Davis, David Brion, 77n25
Davis, Dr. Elizabeth B., 73
Deale, James, 41
Deanne, James V., 20

Delaware, xxii
Dickerson, Dennis, 73
Dinah (enslaved woman), 45
Dinah (free woman), 38
District of Columbia, 39, 50
domestic servants, 6, 8, 56–57, 61
domestic slave trade, 5, 52; secondary, 18
Dorchester County, xx
Dorsey, Jennifer Hull, 4, 46, 55, 58, 61, 64
Dorsey, Rachel, 65
Dorsey, Samuel, 65
Douglass, Frederick, xx, 7, 9, 20, 23, 44, 54; Annapolis museum, 68, 73; Capitol statue of, xx; church dedication, 68
Dred Scott decision (1846), 39
Du Bois, W. E. B., 70
Duke of Gloucester Street (Annapolis), xix, 68
Dulany, Daniel, 17, 21, 22
Dulany, Lloyd, 10
Dulany, Rebecca Tasker, 22
Dulany family, 9, 22, 45, 81n62
Dunbar, Erica Armstrong, 3
Dutch West India Company, 36

Eastern Shore, 9, 55, 56, 58, 63, 64
East St. Louis (Ill.), 70
education, 63–64, 65
Edwards, Laura F., 29
Egerton, Douglas, 29
elderly kin, 57–58
Elizabeth (enslaved child), 44
Ellen (freedom petitioner), 36–37
Ellicott City, 51
emancipation (formal), 38. *See also* freedom petitions; manumission
Emancipation Proclamation (1863), xx
Enfield Chase Plantation, 21
England. *See* Britain, anti-slavery measures
enslaved women: "afterlife" of slavery and, 12; agency and, 6, 7, 14, 29, 55; boundaries with freedom of, xxii, 1–13, 41; family and, 7, 20–21; forms of protest by, 7; freedom petitions by, 26, 27–40; freedom purchases for, 46–48; freedom tactics of, 74; invisibility of, 3; manumission and (*see* manumission); mobility and, 2, 7–11, 12, 13; oral genealogy preservation by, 27, 32; paucity of material about, xxi, xxii, 3; reproductive value of, 1, 7, 12, 14–26, 27; sexual exploitation of, 7, 12, 15–18, 22, 23–26, 61; strength cultivation by, 19, 74; studies of, 3–4; three tactics in quest for freedom of, 74; types of work performed by, 6, 8–10, 56–57, 61. *See also* mothers
entail, 18, 48, 80n32
Episcopal Church, xviii, 11, 70, 73
escaped slaves, xx, 23, 45, 50
Evina (slave child), 48
extended family, 12, 19, 20, 39, 57, 85n58

faith, 74
family: as Akan cultural marker, 44; black men's legal exclusion from, 55; enslavement and freedom coexistent in, 12, 42; enslavement threats to, 7, 18, 20; extended, 12, 19, 20, 39, 57, 85n58 (*see also* networks); free blacks and, xvii–xviii, 13, 41, 48–49, 50, 55, 61, 63; freedom linked with access to, 40, 41; freedom purchases for, 46–52; generational transmission of stories about, 23; guardianships and, 57–58; hiring out and, 44–45; importance to African Americans of, 51; industrial slavery as strain on, 9; manumitted women and, 37, 41, 46, 47, 51, 54; Maryland slaves' relative stability of, 21; matrifocal/matrilocal systems of, 20, 54, 57; networks and, 7, 85n58 (*see also* kinship ties); oral genealogy and, 27, 32; private farm plots and, 44; reunifications of, 46–47, 49; slave formation/maintenance of, 6–7, 20–21, 26, 55; as slaveholder's property, 50; slave sale breakup of, 20, 21; women's efforts for survival of, 40, 41. *See also* households
"fancy trade," 23
Fanny (purchaser of own freedom), 47, 48
farming, 4–5, 8, 44, 45
fathers: of children of manumitted women, 37, 54; child's slave status and, 16; separation of, from child, 51; slavery's marginalization of, 20; stepfathers as, 57
Faulkner, Benjamin, 65
Fells Point (Baltimore area), xx, 56
female-headed households, 13, 57, 66
feminist consciousness, 3–4
Fen, Jenet, 18
fictive kin, 20, 55, 57, 85n58
Fields, Barbara, 4–5

INDEX

Fisher, Ann, 31
Folks, Charity, xvii–xxii, 4, 11–13; Annapolis and, 5, 8, 22, 26, 55, 60, 68, 73; background and significance of, xvii–xviii, 22–23; birth of, xvii, 21–22, 68; burial site and headstone of, 67–68, 70, 74; children of, xvii, 6, 8, 13, 25–26, 42–44, 53, 56, 59, 74; children's manumission negotiated by, 26, 51–52; children's sibling rivalry and, 56, 59–60; community and, 42; current remembrances for, 73; death of, xvii; descendants' legacy, xvii–xviii, xix–xx, 63, 69–71, 73–74; extended family network of, 12; family residence and, 55; final years of, 67; freedom's meaning to, 6, 11, 42; freedom tactics of, 74; grandchildren of, 4, 12, 53, 54, 58, 70, 74; great-grandchildren of, 65, 70, 74; herbal medicine and, 8–9; historical obscurity of, xx; household of, as free woman, 13, 53, 54; husband of, 10, 26, 42, 52, 56; last public documentation of life of, 67; manumission document of, xvii, xix, 42–43, 51–52; manumission process and, 4, 12, 41, 42, 51–52, 55; mobility of, 7–9, 12, 45; parentage of, 21–22, 25, 42; plays about, 73; property ownership by, xvii, 60, 68, 70; religious belief and, 11; Ridout household and, 8, 9, 22, 26, 60, 61, 62, 67; slaveholding by, 61–62; symbolism of life of, xxi; wealth amassed by, xxii, 60, 62, 69; will of, 62; womanist strategies of, 22–23
Folks, Elizabeth (Charity's granddaughter), 56, 60–61, 62
Folks, Hannah (Charity's daughter), 26, 42, 52, 56
Folks, Henry (Thomas's son), 26, 56
Folks, Lil' Charity (Charity's daughter). *See* Bishop, Charity Folks
Folks, Mary (Charity's daughter). *See* Lake, Mary Folks Norris
Folks, Thomas (Tom; Charity's husband), 10, 26, 42, 52, 53, 56, 59; headstone of, 67–68, 71, 74; slaveholders of, 68; slaveholding by, 61–62; as stepfather, 57
Folks, Thomas (Tom's grandson), 56
forges, 45
Fourteenth Amendment, 2
Francis, Thomas, 65
Franklin Street (Annapolis), 68

Frederick County, 39
Frederick Douglass–Isaac Myers Maritime Park, xx
free blacks, xxi–xxii, 4–7, 9, 10, 23; age of manumission and, 36; Annapolis and, xviii, 55, 56, 61, 65; Baltimore and, xviii, 4, 36, 55–56, 63, 65; barriers for, 61, 63–65, 66; beige aristocracy of, 63; children's apprenticeships and, 13, 50, 53, 54, 55, 63–66; *Dred Scott* decision and, 39; family freedom purchases by, 41, 48–49, 50; female-male ratio of, 2, 56; feminist consciousness and, 3–4; guardianships and, 57–59; households of, 13, 53, 54, 55–60, 66; intact families and, 38; Liberian colonization movement and, 39, 58–59; male family roles and, 54, 55, 57–58; male occupations and, 61; manumitted interracial children as, 15; Maryland population of, xxi, 4, 40, 51, 55–58, 59, 61, 63; prominent families of, xvii–xviii, 63; property holding by, 54, 61–62, 69–70; restrictions on, 59, 63, 66; slave contacts with, 11, 45; as slaveholders, 61, 61–62; southern legal exclusion of, 37–38; surname "Freeman" chosen by, 29; wage labor market and, 55, 56–57, 60–61; wealth of, xxii, 2, 61, 62, 65, 69–70; white racism and, 61, 63, 69; women's agency and, 6, 40, 54, 57
freedom, xxii, 1–13, 29–40; "afterlife of slavery" concept and, 12; certificates of, 63; community and, 41–52; as concept and reality, 7; conditions for grants of, 39; for future generations, 12, 40, 74; heritability of, 40; households and, 53–66; via manumission (*see* manumission); mobility and, 7–13; as multifaceted, 13; via petition (*see* freedom petitions); purchases of, 4, 10, 12, 44, 46–50, 51–52; racial identity and, 16, 39; resettlement in Liberia and, 39, 58, 59; social justice and, 66; women's three tactics and, 74
freedom petitions, 12, 27–40, 50; costs of process of, 30; court challenges and, 26; enslaved women's formal use of, 26, 27–28, 40; first in new United States, 29; lengthy process of, 30–31; Maryland 1809 law and, 12, 35, 36, 37; mother's status as basis of, 26,

freedom petitions (*continued*)
27–29, 30–40; status of future children and, 35; violent retaliations to, 30
free labor market. *See* wage labor
Freeman, Elizabeth ("Mum Bett"), 29
French colonial slave owners, 23, 33. *See also* Haitian Revolution
Frey, Sylvia, 3
Fuente, Alejandro de la, 29
fugitive slaves, xx, 23, 45, 50

Galloway, John, 17, 20
Gambia, xi
Garner, Margaret, xvii, 19
Gassamay, Mary, 48
Gate Street (Annapolis), 55
Gedney, Solomon, 37
gender: apprenticeship arrangements and, 64, 66; bids for freedom and, 7; child's slave status and, 16; family responsibilities and, 54, 55; free black ratio, 2, 56; heads of household and, 13, 57, 66; manhood concept, 58; as manumission factor, 4, 7; manumission of children and, 10; migrants to Liberia and, 58; mobility and, 8; oppression and, 14; poverty and, 54, 66; property ownership laws and, 18, 62, 80n32; slave labor and, 5, 8; white male privilege, 16; white women's jealousy of slave mistresses, 18; womanhood definition, 22–23. *See also* enslaved women; fathers; mothers
genealogy, 19, 27, 32
Georgetown University, founders of, 32
Ghana, xix, 41, 43–44
Gibson, Horatio Samuel, 48
Glymph, Thavolia, 6, 7, 18
Gold Coast, xix, 41, 43–44
Gordon-Reed, Annette, 25
Green, William, 47
Griffith, Sally, 45
Grimké family, xviii
Grivno, Max, 4, 6

Haitian Revolution, 3, 5, 23, 33, 77n25
Haley, Alex, 68–69, 73; *Roots*, xx
Haley, Christopher, 68
Hammond, Caroline, 50

Hammond, Rezin, 36–37
Hampton Plantation, 8, 23, 61
Harlem, N.Y., 70
Harlem Hospital Center, Psychiatry Department, 70
Harrison, Araminta, 48
Harrison, King, 34
Hartman, Saidiya, 12
Hawkins, Susanna, 46
Hayes-Williams, Janice, xix, xx, 73
Hemings, Sally, xvii, 25
Henry, James, 48
Henry, Sally, 39
herbal medicine, 8–9, 19, 43
Hink, William, 65
hiring out, 10, 44–45
Historic Annapolis Foundation, 69
Hodes, Martha, 32
Hood, Eliza, 48
Hood, Elizabeth, 47–48
Hood, Hester, 47–48
hope, 74
households, 53–66; female-headed, 13, 57, 66; as gathering place, 55, 57; kinship ties and, 56, 58; multigenerational, 53; traditional male-headed, 58
Howard, George, 49
Howard, Maria, 49
Howard, Mary Ann, 49
Howard, Philip, 49
Howard, Ruth, 49
Hurt, John, 20

indentured women, 31
indigenous people, slave children of, 28, 34, 39
infanticide, 19
infant mortality rates, 19
informational networks, 45
inheritance: entail and, 18, 62, 80n32; of slaves, 18, 35, 36–37, 42, 61; of slave status, 12, 14, 15–16, 18–19, 21, 24–25, 31, 35–37, 51
intermarriage, definition of, 49. *See also* interracial sex
international slave trade: British ban on, 14, 32–33; Middle Passage and, 16–17, 41, 43; Tasker family and, 81n62; U.S. constitutional ending of, 35
interracial sex: black man–white woman

consequences of, 16, 31; enslaved woman–slave owner, 7, 12, 15–18, 22–26, 61; enslaved woman–white man marriage, 49–50; jealousy of slave mistress, 18; offspring's manumission and, 15, 25
Irish immigrants, 31, 47
ironworks, 9
Isabella (enslaved woman), 48

Jack (slave), 42
Jackson, Harriet (Charity's daughter). *See* Calder, Harriet Jackson
Jackson, James (Charity's son), 26, 42, 56, 57; manumission of, 51, 52; resentments felt by, 59, 60
Jacksonian democracy, 5
Jamaica, 14, 17
James Somerset v. Charles Stewart (1772; Britain), 32, 33
Jefferson, Thomas, 25
Jenifer, Daniel St. Thomas, 49
Jennison (slaveholder), 29
Jesuits, 33
Johns, Clem, 64
Johns, James, 64
Johns, Kinsey, 64
Johnson, Anna, 48
Johnson, Betsey, 47
Johnson, Cassandra, 47
Johnson, Evey, 47
Johnson, George, 48–49
Johnson, James Weldon, 70
Johnson, Mary, 48–49
Johnson, Milly, 47
Johnson, Samuel, 65
Johnson, Walter, 6
Joice, Ann, 32, 34
Jones, Catherine, 64
Jones Falls (Baltimore area), 56
Journal of African American History, xx
Juliet (enslaved woman), 48
jumping the broom, 20, 56

Kent Island, 51
King, Wilma, 54
kinship ties, 20, 27, 37, 40, 50, 51, 56, 57, 58, 85n58
Ku Klux Klan, 69

Kunta Kinte, xx, 68
Kunta Kinte–Alex Haley Foundation, 68, 69

lactation, 8, 21
Lafargue mental health clinic (Harlem), 70
Lake, Mary Folks Norris (Charity's daughter), 26, 42, 52, 71; rivalry with Lil' Charity, 56, 59–60; two marriages of, 56
Lake, Moses (Charity's son-in-law), 56, 60
laundresses, 55, 60
Lavinia (free woman), 38
Lee, Anne, 48
Lee, Henry, 48
Lee, Patty, 48
legal personhood, 40
Leone, Mark, xviii–xix, 11
Levering, Sarah, 19, 51
Lewis, Perry, 51
Liberia, 39, 58, 59
liberty. *See* freedom
Louisiana Purchase (1803), 23
love, meaning of, 74
Lowe, Enoch, 30
Lucy (enslaved woman), 46
Lurena (freedom petitioner), 36–37

Machubin, Elizabeth (Burke), 18
Machubin, William, 38
Macks, Richard, 18
Mahoney, Charles, 32, 33, 64
Mahoney, Daniel, 33
Mahoney, Patrick, 32, 33
manhood, concept of, 58
Mansfield, Lord, 32
manumission, xviii, xx, 1–2, 4–7, 23–25; agency and, 6; after childbearing years, 7; children and, 10, 12, 15, 24–25, 36, 46–47, 48; children's apprenticeship and, 13, 50, 63–66; class divisions and, 60; as complicated negotiation, 41; considerations concerning, 10–12, 13, 28, 42; diverse approaches to, 7, 50; economic incentives against, 36; economic status of, 63; enslavement years prior to, 46; exile conditions of, 39; family ties and, 37, 41, 46, 47, 51, 54; free wage economy and, 53, 60–63; gender as factor in, 4, 7; generational legal challenges of, 37; group, 46, 51; of interracial offspring, 15,

manumission (*continued*)
24–25; issuance of deeds and, 49; legacies of slavery and, 54; by sexual relations with slaveholder, 23; state laws and, 10–11, 12, 16, 24, 25, 36, 37; statistics, 47; by will or testament, 10–11, 18, 25, 36–37, 39, 42, 49. *See also* freedom; freedom petitions
market economy, 9–10, 45, 46. *See also* wage labor
marriage, 32, 49–50; denial to slaves of, 17; enslaved women as owners' mistresses and, 23; freedom and, 54, 56; intermarriage definition, 49; meaning of, for slave women, 17, 20; slave "jumping the broom" custom, 20, 56; slaves as white women's dowry, 10, 52
Martiner, Joseph Corbel, 10
Maryland, xix, xxi–xxii, 17, 22, 50; acts concerning slavery, 10–11, 12; African American official heritage museum, 68; African origin of slaves brought to, 41, 43; atonements for slavery, 68–69; capital of (*see* Annapolis); communal vision of freedom and, 41–42; domestic slave trade and, 52; entailment of slave children and, 18; fluid black population of, xx; formal apology for slavery (2007), 69; free black population of, xxi, 4, 40, 51, 55–58, 59, 61, 63; freedom petition suits in, 28, 29, 30–40; Haitian Revolution's legal influence on, 33; interracial sex law of, 16; large slaveholding families of, 47, 81n62; Liberian resettlement campaign and, 39, 58; manumission and, xviii, xx, 4–7, 10, 51; orphans' court function and, 65; slave families relative stability in, 21; slavery's ghosts in, 68–69; slaves as property ruling in, 35; three historically prominent slaves from, xx. *See also specific cities, counties, and places*
Maryland Colonization Society, 58
Maryland General Court of the Western Shore, 30–31, 34
Maryland Historic Trust, Office of Research, Survey, and Registration, xix
Maryland State Archives, xix, xx
Maryland State House, 68
matrifocal/matrilocal systems, 20, 54, 57, 85n58
McTavish, Emily, 21

Mercer, Margaret, 57
Methodist Church, xviii, 11
middle ground, 13
Middle Passage, 16–17, 41, 43
midwives, 8
Milly (enslaved woman), 42
Minsky, Jane, 24, 47
Mitchell, Michelle, 59
mobility, 7–11, 12, 13, 44, 45–46; meanings of, 2; opportunities from, 8
Montreal, Québec, 3
moral mother, 14
Morgan, Philip D., 8
Mote, C. D., Jr., 79
mothers, 13, 42–45, 54; enslaved women's value as, 1, 12, 14–27; family creation by (*see* family); freedom petitions based on race of, 26, 27–29, 30–40; freedom purchases of, 47–48; infanticide by, 19; poverty and, 66; realities of enslavement and, 19–23, 44–45; resistance modeling by, 22–23; status of children born to (*see* children); status of slave versus free, 34, 35; status of white versus black, 14, 31. *See also* reproduction
Mount Mariah African Methodist Episcopal Church (Annapolis), 68
Moynihan, Daniel Patrick, 13
Mullin, Richard, 47
Mullin, Susanna, 47
Murray, Hannah, 56
Mustakeem, Sowande, 16–17
Myers, Amrita Chakrabarti, 6, 38, 54

Nail, John, 70
Nathan, Sydney, 41
National Register of Historic Places, 68
National Slavery Museum (proposed), 69
National Underground Railroad Freedom Center (Cincinnati), 69
Native American women, descent from, 28, 34, 39
"Negro Catherine" (enslaved woman), 64
"Negro Charles" (enslaved man), 31
Negro Family, The (Moynihan), 13
Negro in the American Revolution, The (Quarles), 3
"Negro Joe" (enslaved man), 38
networks, 7, 40–43, 58; freedom purchase

INDEX

and, 47, 50, 52; manumission and, 40, 41; mobility and, 12, 43; types of, 85n58. *See also* kinship ties
New Amsterdam, 36
New England, 3, 28, 29
New Orleans, 10, 23
New York, 37, 70
Norris, Edward, 65
Norris, Julia, 65
Norris, Phillip, 56
Northampton Furnace and Ironworks, 9
Norton, Mary Beth, 3

Ogle, Anne Tasker, 22, 25, 81n62
Ogle, Mary. *See* Ridout, Mary Ogle
Ogle, Samuel, 20, 21, 22
Ogle family, 26, 81n62
Ogleton, Letty (mother), freedom petition of, 27–28, 29, 30, 31
Ogleton, Maria (maternal ancestor), 28
Ogleton children (Henry, Lucky, Lucy, Michael, Sarah), 27–28, 30, 31
"On Agency" (W. Johnson), 6
oral tradition, 31–32, 43; genealogy, 27, 32
orphans' courts, 11, 50, 63, 64, 66; function of, 65

Papenfuse, Eric, 32–33
Pargas, Damian Alan, 6, 44
partus sequitur ventrem (status of child follows mother), 51
Patterson, Orlando, 41
Patton, Dorothy, 73
Paul, St., 1, 14, 27, 41, 53, 67, 74
Paul, Isaac, 49
Penningroth, Dylan, 44
Pennington, James W., 18
Pennsylvania, xxii
pensions, 46, 60
personhood, legal, 40
petitions. *See* freedom petitions
Pettibone, Charles, 49
Philadelphia, 3, 56–57
Phillips, Christopher, 5
plaçage system, 23
plantation slaves: movement among, 10; urban slave advantage over, 9–10
Pleck, Elizabeth H., 3, 28

Potomac River, 10
poverty: apprenticeship as guard against, 64–65; free black women and, 54, 66; gendered perception of, 66; relief system, 65
pregnancy. *See* reproduction
Prince George's County Court, 27–28
property: African American notion of, 44, 51; African concept of family as, 52; enslaved people as, 14, 17–18, 27, 38, 39, 51; entail and, 18, 48, 80n32; free black holders of, xvii, 54, 60, 61–62, 66, 68, 69–70; free black purchases of family members as, 50; implications of people as, 43, 45, 46; personhood suits and, 30; transition to freedom and, 29, 30, 51; white female restricted ownership of, 18, 62, 80n32
pro-slavery texts, 51
prostitutes, 61
Prout, Kitty, 48
Pybus, Cassandra, 3

Quakers, 30
Quarles, Benjamin, 3
Queen, Edward, 33
Queen Nannie, xviii

Rachel (enslaved woman), 47, 48
racism, 61, 63, 69
Randall, Thomas, 20
rape, 12, 15, 17, 18
Rashad, Liberty, 73–74
real estate ownership, 61, 62, 66, 70
Reconciliation March (2004), 68
Reconstruction period, 52, 66
religion, 4, 9, 11, 43, 59, 74
reproduction: enslaved women midwives, 8; enslaved women's birth control efforts, 19, 80n36; enslavement of offspring, 12, 18–19, 21, 31, 35–36, 37, 51; entail and, 18; high slave birth rates, 16; Maryland law concerning, 12, 35, 37, 39; maternal health, 16–17; as only legal way of obtaining new slaves, 36, 37, 40; racial slavery linked with, 34–35, 39, 40; valuation of enslaved woman's potential, 1, 7, 12, 14–26. *See also* children; mothers
resistance, 6, 7, 19–26; enslaved mothers and, 14–15, 19, 22–23, 25; fugitive slaves and, xx, 23, 45, 50; slave rebellions, 3, 5, 37

revolution. *See* Age of Revolution; American Revolution; Haitian Revolution
Reynolds, Alexander, 50
Reynolds, Elizabeth, 49, 50
Reynolds, John, 50
Reynolds, William, 49–50
Reynolds Tavern, 68
Ridgely, Charles, 9, 23
Ridgely family, 81n62
Ridout, Barbara, xix
Ridout, Horatio, 22, 49, 52, 60
Ridout, John, xix, 45; Annapolis home of, 22, 68, 73; Annapolis row houses of, 11, 55; burial site of, 67; death and will of, 42, 60; manumission of Charity and her children by, 42; marriage to Mary Ogle of, 10, 22, 51; pension provision for Charity by, 60
Ridout, John (descendant), 68
Ridout, Dr. John (grandson), 61, 62
Ridout, Mary Ogle, xix, 42, 52; bequest to Charity from, 60; burial site of, 67; manumission of Charity's family by, 51, 52, 53, 62; marriage of, 10, 22, 51
Ridout, Mollie, 69
Ridout, Orlando, IV (Lannie), xix, xx, 62, 69
Ridout, Orlando, V, 19
Ridout, Samuel, 22, 52, 60, 62
Ridout family, xx, 5, 47; Annapolis houses of, xix, 8, 11, 22, 26, 55, 68, 73; Charity's positions with, 8, 9, 22, 26, 60, 61, 62, 67; prominence of, 52; racial reconciliation efforts by 68, 69
Ringgold, Thomas, 20
Roberts, Dorothy, 66
Rockman, Seth, 56, 57, 61
Roots (A. Haley), xx
runaway slaves. *See* fugitive slaves
Russo, Jean, xx
Russwurm, John, 58
Ruth (enslaved woman), 42, 60

Saillant, John, 59
Saint-Domingue, 30, 33. *See also* Haitian Revolution
Schermerhorn, Calvin, 4, 47
Schwartz, Marie Jenkins, 17
Schweninger, Loren, 2, 27, 30, 32
Scott, Dred, 39
Scott, Upton, 31

Scurlock, Joan, xix–xx, 73
seamstresses, 8
serial marriage, 20
service professions, 61
Settle, Josiah T., 70
Settle, Teresa Vogelsang (Charity's great-granddaughter), 70
Severn River, 67
sexual exploitation, 7, 12, 15–18, 22–26, 61; strategies against, 22–23
Shango (orisha), 11
shoemakers, 61
Shorter family, 32
Silent Protest Parade (1917; Harlem), 70
Silver, Gail, 73
skin color, 7; class consciousness and, 63; distancing from blackness, 28; manumission grants and, 28, 29, 34, 35; slave status linked with, 16, 28, 39
slaveholders: African Americans as, 61–62; Baltimore society of, 8, 23–24, 81n62; control over children of manumitted women by, 36; employment of free blacks by, 61; family connections of slaves with, 28, 50; hiring out of slaves by, 44–45; inheritance of slaves and, 18, 35, 36–37, 42, 61; large Maryland families of, 47, 81n62; manumission by (*see* manumission); property concept of, 14, 17–18, 27, 38, 39, 50, 51; sexual exploitation by, 7, 12, 15–18, 22–26, 61; value of highly fertile women to, 17
slave rebellions, 3, 5, 37
slavery: African birthplace of, 41; "afterlife" of, 12; Akan people's view of, 43; belief system of, 11; "blackness" basis of, 16, 28, 39; British illegality of, 32, 77n25; decreasing profitability of, 4; family and (*see* family); as hereditary, 13, 15–16, 31, 36, 38; hiring out and, 10, 44–45; legacies of, 54, 68–69; marginalization of fathers by, 20; Maryland's atonements for, 68–69; perpetuation through natural reproduction of, 1, 15–16, 36, 37, 40; plantation versus urban, 9–10; as social death, 41; texts supporting, 51; Thirteenth Amendment ending, 2. *See also* enslaved women
slave trade, domestic, 5, 18, 52. *See also* international slave trade
Slayton House (Annapolis), 11

Smith, Charlotte, 9
Smith, Lucy, 9
Smith, Martha, 45
Snowden, John, 9
Snowden, Samuel, 50
Snowden, Thomas, 50
Snowden, Viney, 50
Snowden family, 9, 47, 81n62
Snowden Ironworks, 9
social contract, 66
social responsibility, 13, 66
South, 37, 61
South Carolina, 29, 38
Spanish slave societies, 23, 29, 46
Sparrow, James, 57
Sparrow, Nelly, 57
spiritual gifts, 9, 11, 43, 74
Sprigg, Richard, 21
St. Anne's Cemetery (Annapolis), 67–68, 70–71, 73–74
stepfathers, 57
St. Mary's Catholic Church (Annapolis), 73
St. Mary's County, 31–32
St. Mary's Parish Church (Baltimore), 70
St. Philip's Episcopal Church (Harlem), 70, 73
Struse, Clayton, 73
Study for the Legacy of Slavery in Maryland Project, 68

Talbot County, 57, 64
Tasker, Anne (Ogle), 22, 25, 81n62
Tasker, Anne Bladen, 81n62
Tasker, Benjamin, Sr., 21, 22, 81n62
Tasker, Rebecca (Dulany), 22
Tasker family, 9, 26, 81n62
Tennessee, 70
Thirteenth Amendment, 2
Thomas, Robert, 20
tobacco farming, 4–5; shift to wheat, 8
Toogood, Eleanor, 31
Toogood, Maria, 64
Toussaint L'Ouverture, 3
travel. *See* mobility
Trussell, Dr. Elizabeth Bishop Davis (Charity's great-great-great granddaughter), 70
Truth, Sojourner, xvii, 17, 19, 37
Tubman, Harriet, xx, 7, 19
Tulip Hill Plantation, 17
Turner, Nat, 37

Turner, Sasha, 14, 17
Tydings, Sophia, 37–38

underground railroad, 69
University of Maryland, xviii, 69

Vanderbilt University, 73
Van Wagenen, Isabella. *See* Truth, Sojourner
Van Wagenen, Peter, 37
"Velia, a slave," xviii
violence, 12, 15, 17, 18, 21–22, 25
Virginia, 15, 69; entail practice, 80n32; free black population, xxii; freedom petition suits, 31; hereditary slavery law (1662), 51; interracial sex law, 16; Turner slave rebellion, 37
Vogelsang, Charity Bishop (Charity's granddaughter), 74
Vogelsang, Peter, 70
Vogelsang, Rebecca Bishop (Charity's granddaughter), 70, 74
Vogelsang, Teresa (Settle; Charity's great-granddaughter), 70

wage labor, 44–46; competition with white workers and, 61; free black males and, 61; free black women and, 50, 55, 56–57, 60–63; hiring out of slaves and, 10, 44–45; manumitted women and, 53–54
Walker, David, 59
Walker, Mary, 41
Walker, Quok, 29
Wallace, Barbara, 55
Walters, Delores M., 21
Ward, Anne, 23
Ward, Samuel Ringgold, 23
Ware, Francis, 17
War of 1812, 5
War of Independence. *See* American Revolution
washerwomen, 55
Washington, D.C., 39, 50
wealth, free black, xxii, 2, 61, 62, 65, 69–70
Weems, David, 34
welfare system, 11
Wells, Ida B., 70
Wesley, Marylyn C., 53
West River Farm, 21
wet nurses, 8

wheat farming, 8
White, Deborah Gray, 19; *Ar'n't I a Woman?*, 3
Whitman, T. Stephen, 32, 36, 55, 63
Williams, Heather Andrea, 41, 52
Williams, Robert, 38
Williams, Rose, 17
Williams, Susannah, 38
wills, 10–11, 18, 25, 36–37, 39, 42, 49, 60, 62
women. *See* enslaved women; gender; mothers; reproduction

Worthington family, 45
Wright, James, 64
Wright, Perry, 49
Wright family, xviii
Wye Plantation, 20

Yealdhall, Nanny, 64
Yoruba religion, 11

Zipf, Karen, 66

RACE IN THE ATLANTIC WORLD, 1700–1900

*The Hanging of Angélique: The Untold Story of Canadian
Slavery and the Burning of Old Montréal*
    BY AFUA COOPER

Christian Ritual and the Creation of British Slave Societies, 1650–1780
    BY NICHOLAS M. BEASLEY

*African American Life in the Georgia Lowcountry:
The Atlantic World and the Gullah Geechee*
    EDITED BY PHILIP MORGAN

*The Horrible Gift of Freedom:
Atlantic Slavery and the Representation of Emancipation*
    BY MARCUS WOOD

*The Life and Letters of Philip Quaque,
the First African Anglican Missionary*
    EDITED BY VINCENT CARRETTA AND TY M. REESE

*In Search of Brightest Africa: Reimagining the Dark
Continent in American Culture, 1884–1936*
    BY JEANNETTE EILEEN JONES

*Contentious Liberties: American Abolitionists in
Post-emancipation Jamaica, 1834–1866*
    BY GALE L. KENNY

*We Are the Revolutionists: German-Speaking Immigrants
and American Abolitionists after 1848*
    BY MISCHA HONECK

The American Dreams of John B. Prentis, Slave Trader
    BY KARI J. WINTER

*Missing Links: The African and American Worlds of
R. L. Garner, Primate Collector*
    BY JEREMY RICH

Almost Free: A Story about Family and Race in Antebellum Virginia
    BY EVA SHEPPARD WOLF

*To Live an Antislavery Life: Personal Politics and the
Antebellum Black Middle Class*
    BY ERICA L. BALL

*Flush Times and Fever Dreams: A Story of Capitalism and
Slavery in the Age of Jackson*
    BY JOSHUA D. ROTHMAN

Diplomacy in Black and White: John Adams, Toussaint Louverture, and Their Atlantic World Alliance
    BY RONALD ANGELO JOHNSON

Enterprising Women: Gender, Race, and Power in the Revolutionary Atlantic
    BY KIT CANDLIN AND CASSANDRA PYBUS

Eighty-Eight Years: The Long Death of Slavery in the United States, 1777–1865
    BY PATRICK RAEL

Finding Charity's Folk: Enslaved and Free Black Women in Maryland
    BY JESSICA MILLWARD

The Mulatta Concubine: Terror, Intimacy, Freedom, and Desire in the Black Transatlantic
    BY LISA ZE WINTERS